M000077785

I'm Glad You Asked

I'm Glad You Asked

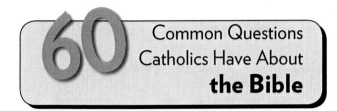

60 Common Questions
Catholics Have About
the Bible

Fr. Mark R. Pierce

Saint Mary's Press®

Nihil Obstat: Rev. Robert S. Horihan, STL
Censor Librorum
November 13, 2007

Imprimatur: †Most Rev. Bernard J. Harrington, DD
Bishop of Winona
November 13, 2007

The nihil obstat and imprimatur are official declarations that a book or pamphlet is free of doctrinal or moral error. No implication is contained therein that those who have granted the nihil obstat or imprimatur agree with the contents, opinions, or statements expressed, nor do they assume any legal responsibility associated with publication.

The publishing team included Brian Singer-Towns, development editor; Lorraine Kilmartin, reviewer; prepress and manufacturing coordinated by the production departments of Saint Mary's Press.

Printed in the United States of America

3459

ISBN 978-0-88489-975-4

Library of Congress Cataloging-in-Publication Data

Pierce, Mark R.
    I'm glad you asked : 60 common questions Catholics have about the Bible / Mark R. Pierce.
    p. cm.
ISBN 978-0-88489-975-4 (pbk.)
    1. Bible—Miscellanea. 2. Catholic Church—Doctrines. I. Title.

BS612.P544 2008
220.6'1024282—dc22

                                                    2007041269

Dedication

To my students at all levels,
who have been honest enough to have questions
and brave enough to voice them.
Without them *neither* they nor I would have learned much.

Contents

Note: Some of the questions in the table of contents are shorter versions of the actual questions in the book.

Section 3: FAQs on Challenges About the Catholic Faith

Introduction

My parents were shepherds. Well, they didn't actually raise sheep, but in some ways, they were like the shepherds in the Christmas story from the Gospel of Luke. Minding their own business, the shepherds got a visit from a very talkative angel (complete with a heavenly backup group) who announced that God was coming to live among them as a newborn child in the next town. For my folks, their religious faith seemed quite natural, like breathing. Like the shepherds, their trust in God was bedrock; they never asked questions.

I, however, am an astrologer. Well, not *really*, but in some ways, I'm like the magi in the Nativity story from the Gospel of Matthew, who were astrologers from the East. The magi had a long journey, following a star that faded on them at a critical moment. They studied a lot, asked questions, and depended on others for directions. I don't mean to sound overly dramatic, but though I received my faith from my folks, unlike them I've always asked, "Why?" and "How?" and "Where does it say that?" I must have driven them nuts. But they put up with it, out of their love for God . . . and me.

It seems that there are many more astrologers in the world than shepherds these days. Young people often drop by my office or send me an e-mail and ask "Why?" and "How?" and "Where does it say that?" about faith. If it drives me a little nuts, it's only fair. Most of the questions I hear are about how to read the Bible, how to make sense of hard-to-understand Scripture verses, and how to explain our faith to non-Catholic friends. I've gathered sixty of those questions, grouped them into those three categories, and tried my best to make sense of them, one astrologer to another. I'd be pleased if they help you reach your destination.

Section 1: FAQs About Using the Bible

"This will change your life!" How often have you heard that line before? A new cell phone plan, the choice of a college, psychic hotlines—lots of things get pitched to us in such breathless tones. And we have all been disappointed. No wonder we've all become a little suspicious of sales talk.

So what makes me think I'm justified in pitching the Bible to you this way? Well, exhibit A would be the large number of people, past and present, who swear their lives have indeed been changed by reading it. I am one of them. I was a little late catching on, but I have come to see that God's Word is powerful, life-changing stuff. I bet someone close to you can give her or his own testimonial. (Hint: think of the person who may have given you this book or who assigned [sigh!] you to read it.)

But, truth be told, for every person who finds the Bible engrossing the first time he or she picks it up, there are bunches of folks who initially find it mystifying. And then there are others who, when they're being honest, admit they just find it boring. In my experience, the problem is not with the Bible itself, or even the motivation of the reader, but rather is a matter of "mechanics." Beginners get their hopes smashed because they don't know where to begin reading the Bible or what to make of what they find when they do.

I'd like to help you avoid that. This first section of this book is a guide to cracking open this big and sometimes intimidating thing called the Bible by way of sixteen questions and answers. Most of these concerns come from actual young people, though I confess to having made up a couple of the questions just to get some things off my chest. You should be able to skip around and read the questions you're interested in and ignore the rest without too much damage to your train of thought.

But before you plow into the questions themselves, you might pause and consider the marvel that is writing itself. We take reading and writing for granted, but putting down letters to make words was a big step forward for our ancestors. It allowed them (and allows us) to capture thoughts, events, and experiences so they can be preserved, revisited, or shared. Now some writing is just a way of holding on to data—a phone book or a dictionary, for example. But sometimes we express ourselves through these little symbols so we can touch people far away (in distance or time, or both) or so they can touch us. Writing and reading is often about relationship.

So when you read the Bible, I hope you have a strong desire to be in relationship with God. We people of faith believe that God authored the Bible—but, as I will explain later, not that God actually wrote it down and faxed it to us. Through the Bible, God wants to be known by us, wants to be encountered. And that, my friend, is why the Bible is well worth every moment of time we can give to it.

How do I get started?

The first time a Bible is put into a person's hands, it's likely quite easy for him or her to make certain assumptions about it—certain *wrong* assumptions. The thinking goes something like this: "Hmm . . . printed pages bound together, cover with a title on it. It looks like a book. The Bible must be a book." But with that understandable conclusion comes certain expectations—the Bible must have a tidy list of returning characters, an orderly progression in time, a single point of view, neat transitions, and helpful summaries for the inattentive reader. I regret to have to be the one to tell you this, but as far as the Bible is concerned, none of these are the case. The Bible isn't a textbook or a romance novel; in fact, it isn't even a book so much as a library, a collection of writings bound together.

Walk into your local library and ask the person at the desk, "Where should I begin?" and she or he will likely smile and start lobbing questions at you: "What are you looking for? What interests you? Do you enjoy history? poetry? philosophy? law? imaginative stories?" Once you tell the person what you are after, she or he can direct you where to find it. A library has it all, and in many ways, so does the Bible. Despite its appearances, the Bible is not a book in the usual sense, but a collection of writings that share a central concern.

This may explain why so many people who are determined to read the Bible start out bravely with Genesis only to run out of gas somewhere in Exodus (if not earlier). They have slipped from a part of the library featuring engaging stories about a remarkable family's escape from slavery to a section that offers chapter after chapter of rules. It's a rough transition.

So the place to start is where your interests lie. Here's a list of entry points for the beginner—a sampling of the kinds of writing you will find in the Bible, in some of their most attractive appearances:

- **Exodus, chapters 1–20:** the dramatic narrative of God's leading the Hebrew slaves to freedom and relationship; the core story of Judaism
- **Second Samuel:** a sober and spicy chronicle of court intrigue during the reign of the great Jewish hero and ancestor of Jesus, David
- **Tobit:** a romantic tale written to encourage the reader to trust in God's watchful care
- **Jonah:** a delightful parable poking fun at us religious people when we think everyone needs a change of heart but us
- **Mark:** the shortest of the Gospels, written to Christians who are finding following Jesus very challenging
- **First Corinthians:** Paul's address to "baby Christians" who are struggling with familiar problems—group squabbles, sex, and worries about what happens when we die
- **First Thessalonians:** maybe the oldest Christian writing in the Bible, encouraging a young church in the face of opposition
- **James:** wise coaching for living the Christian life

2   Why is the Bible so big?

That is a great question, and one I hope you will continue to ask in all your wondering about and seeking after God. The Bible is big because God is big. The flip side is that we human creatures are small (not small as in unimportant, but small as in limited in our ability to get our heads around some things.)

In part the Bible is so large due to *what it tries to communicate*. Explaining a big thing to someone whose understanding is limited sometimes requires lots of words. Then some things are beyond words altogether. How would you attempt to explain the color green to someone blind from birth or the scent of a rose to someone who cannot smell? As helpful as they are, if words can't manage such relatively simple tasks, how will they manage to capture and contain the One who invented green and created a rose's smell?

The Bible itself says as much. In the full version of the Ten Commandments, the Israelites were told not even to try to make an artistic image of God (see Exodus 20:4). Later Moses asked to see God, and God consented—sheltering Moses in a niche in the mountain, then covering the opening with his hand while he passed by: "Then I will remove my hand, so that you may see my back; but my face is not to be seen" (Exodus 33:23). God is not being difficult; it's just hard to drink from a fire hose.

Another thing that makes the Bible big is *how God has chosen to communicate*. Think of the difference between watching a baseball game and perusing the box-score summary, or between viewing an episode of your favorite show and settling for the thumbnail sketch in *TV Guide*. In both cases, the essential information is there, but the very reasons you would tune in to watch—the suspense, the drama, the excitement—are missing. I suppose God *could* have chosen to speak to us via to-do lists, bumper stickers, and sound bytes, but the Scriptures come to us as narratives, poetry, letters, legal codes, and parables because these types of writing do better in drawing us in and making us feel that we are being addressed. Remember, in the end, God's library is less about learning information and more about being in relationship.

So remember that the Bible is big because God speaks to us as he spoke to Moses—at length, in a way we can understand. And the Bible is big because God wants to draw us in to the story as participants, not just observers. And both of those things require lots and lots of words.

3 Why are Catholic Bibles bigger than Protestant Bibles?

As helpful as it might have been, Jesus didn't leave us a reading list. The question of how many books are received as God's written Word has divided Christians for centuries. Though we all have the same twenty-seven writings about the saving work of Jesus (the New Testament), complications arise with the texts we received from the Jewish people. Protestant Christians have thirty-nine books in their Old Testament, Catholics have forty-six, and Orthodox Christians add one or two more.

The biblical library came together slowly and a little untidily. By the end of the second century, a broad consensus on the Church's guiding writings had been reached (with a quibble over one book or another). But this general agreement came apart in the sixteenth century, when Martin Luther placed seven of the Jewish writings that the Church had been using in a separate category, not on the same level as the rest. Other Protestant reformers followed Luther's lead, and in time some publishers stopped printing those writings in their Bibles altogether.* So if a Lutheran friend asks, "Why did you Catholics add those books to the Bible?" it is appropriate to politely respond, "Why did Luther choose to remove them?"

* The books are Judith, Tobit, 1 and 2 Maccabees, Sirach, Wisdom, and Baruch. Protestants place them in a section called the Apocrypha (from a Greek word for "hidden") with other ancient Jewish sacred writings considered not equal to other books in the Bible. The Catholic term for these same seven, fully accepted as God's inspired Word, is *Deuterocanonicals* (from a pair of Greek words meaning "second canon"). All officially approved Catholic Bibles include these books.

4   How is the Bible organized?

It may come as a surprise, especially if you just spent ten minutes searching for a certain passage, but there really is an order to the Bible. It's just not an order that makes automatic sense to modern people. If it were up to us, we might arrange the thing alphabetically (from Amos to Zechariah) or chronologically (in the order of the event or times being discussed). But because of the kind of thing it is, the biblical library is put together more like a cookbook.

Cookbooks aren't arranged alphabetically, but rather by the course of the meal. First come all the drink and punch recipes, then a section with appetizer ideas, then another just for soups, and so on. To find a particular recipe, you could search the index (hoping you have the name of the dish right), or you could just ask, "What sort of food is this?" and then start paging through that particular section until you find the recipe you want.

If you're not into cookbooks, think about a newspaper. On the front page, you will usually find stories reporting the most important events of the day. The author's aim is to inform. Deeper into the paper, you'll come across a section headed "Editorial" or "Opinion." Here the individual authors are trying to persuade you to see things in a new way (well, in his or her way). Keep paging and you will find a sports section, the comics page, and lots and lots of space dedicated to want ads. The newspaper editor could have chosen to scatter these different types of writing throughout the paper, but it is easier for readers to have the same kinds of writings lumped together.

In a similar way, the books in your typical Christian Bible are lumped into smaller collections. The first five (Genesis, Exodus, Leviticus, Numbers, and Deuteronomy) are a special group with its own name: the Pentateuch (which is also called the Torah). Then there's a gathering of books that provide a "God's-eye-view" of what happened when the Chosen People got their own land: the Historical books. Two other collections follow: the Wisdom books and the Prophets. All together, these make up one wing of the biblical library and tell the story of the Jewish people before the coming of Christ—what Christians call the Old Testament. The second wing of the library, the New Testament, begins with four tellings of Jesus's story: the Gospels. The Acts of the Apostles follows, which is the story of Jesus's followers after his Resurrection and Ascension. Then come twenty-one letters by a variety of authors (many by Saint Paul) and then a book of Christian prophecy and encouragement called the Revelation to John.

So when you think about the Bible's organization, don't think of the alphabet or historical order. Think of a cookbook or a newspaper. Like them, the Bible is organized by the kind of writing found in each book.

5 With so many kinds of Bibles, how do I choose one?

Selecting a Bible requires the same savvy you use when purchasing clothes. Enter the Gap and say, "I'd like some jeans," and the clerk will bombard you with questions: "Do you prefer straight leg, boot leg, relaxed fit, regular fit, stonewashed, distressed, regular fly, or button fly?" Before you choose, you need to become familiar with the possibilities. Similarly, God's Word comes packaged in a variety of ways that aim to reach a variety of readers.

Your standard Bible will provide all seventy-three books of God's library between two covers, perhaps with a smattering of extras—cross-references or brief introductions to the individual books.

Add to your standard Bible longer book introductions, lengthy footnotes, sidebar comments on difficult points in the text, maps, and so on, and you have a study Bible. Because, in most cases, the Bible has not been a large part of our growing up, extra help from a study Bible is something I am big on for Catholics.

Devotional Bibles begin again with your standard Bible and often add some of the basic features of a study Bible (maps and introductions). Because this type of Bible is intended to encourage the spiritual growth of the reader, it also includes questions for applying the text to your own life, prayer helps, and even outlines for small-group study. There are devotional Bibles for just about every subgroup and taste: men, women, couples, singles, mothers, teenagers, and so on.

6   What's the best Bible to have?

This may seem like a less-than-helpful answer, but there is no *best* Bible, just Bibles that are better or worse for certain people and certain tasks.

The biblical books were originally written in languages offered by no high school language department I know of: Hebrew, Aramaic, and Greek. So the Bibles we read in English were developed by teams of scholarly translators. If you've studied Spanish or French, you know that there are many ways to translate words from one language to another, with no one of them automatically "the best." Because of this, I steer people away from older English versions (a biblical word for "translations") like the King James Bible or the Douay-Rheims Confraternity Bible. These were very fine Bibles in their time—and can still be beautiful to read—but they were translated nearly four centuries ago, and English has changed a lot since then. When people complain about biblical *thee's* and *thou's,* they aren't really criticizing God's Word, but an outdated translation. For your main Bible, I would suggest you get one translated in the last thirty years.

But locating the best Bible for you also depends on what you want to do with it. For serious study or work in school, a more literal, word-for-word translation is probably better. It may be tougher to understand at first, but the ambiguities and rough spots in the originals are left to stand as they are. For prayer and devotional reading (and with beginners), a freer, thought-for-thought translation is often better, giving the main points without bogging you down along the way. Then there's the matter of biblical bells and whistles—the options and add-ons we talked about in question 5: introductions to the writings, notes, maps, and study questions. Try to be excited by all the variety.

Big-time Bible readers usually have more than one Bible on their shelf. But if you locked me in my closet and demanded a recommendation, I'd steer high school students to an edition of the New American Bible (NAB) or the New Revised Standard Version (NRSV) packaged as *The Catholic Youth Bible*® (Saint Mary's Press, 2005). Both are moderately word-for-word translations with all seventy-three Catholic books, and THE CATHOLIC YOUTH BIBLE includes many study and devotional helps. For younger readers, I'd suggest the Catholic edition* of the Good News Translation (GNT). *Breakthrough! The Bible for Young Catholics* (Saint Mary's Press, 2006) is a GNT that contains many study and devotional aids.

* Catholic editions contain the extra Old Testament books that Catholic readers will want to have. See question 3 in this section.

7 | The Bible seems awfully complex. Why should I want to read it?

I apologize if I'm making the Bible sound overly complex. In a sentence, we should want to read the Bible because it's the inspired, inerrant, canonical revelation of God. Let's take on each of those big words one at a time, starting at the end.

When I say *revelation* here, I'm not talking about the last book of the Bible by that name, but the more general idea of unveiling or opening up. We may get a sense of what someone is like from external clues (her or his clothes, facial expressions, and so on), but to really get to know the person, she or he has to decide to open up to us, let us in, reveal herself or himself.* In the same way, the great God who spun out the universe wants to be known by you and me—not in a vague or bland way, but deeply and personally. The Scriptures are one medium God uses to say, "Let me tell you who I am."

And because God has put so much of himself into the Bible, has been so honest and full in making himself available there, it is proper to say that God is the ultimate author of the Scriptures. This is what we mean when we say the Bible is *inspired*. (There are human authors too, about whom I will speak later).

We trust that God, in love, would always tell us the truth, so a consequence of God's having a hand in producing the Bible is our expectation that it is free from error. That's what *inerrant* means, of course. Having said that, Catholics don't approach the Scriptures as a magic eight-ball that answers every question about science and history, but rather as the truth God wished to be recorded "for the sake of our salvation"[1] (*Catechism of the Catholic Church*, number 107). The Bible contains a good deal of data about history and ancient culture, but what really counts is what the Bible has to say about who God is and who we are, and what God has done and is doing to keep us in friendship (what we mean by salvation). That's what makes it an absolutely trustworthy guide.**

I would imagine the least familiar of these four terms for you is *canonical.* A canon is a ruler or measuring stick. It sets the norm. The list of books we officially accept as making up the Bible, then, is called the canon of Scriptures. And because Catholics expect that God continues to address us through the Spirit, we can use the Bible to test whether our own brainstorms are in accord with God's will. Lay the ruler of what God has spoken in the Bible against your every thought, and the crookedness of what you come up with at times will often be made clear.

I'm not one for lots of memorization, but remembering that the Bible is the inspired, inerrant, canonical revelation of God is a good thing.

* Did you catch that *reveal* is the root of *revelation?*

** This way of thinking about the Bible's inerrancy sets Catholics apart from some Christians. For more about how to understand the inerrancy of God's Word, see questions 8 and 9 in this section.

8   Did God dictate the Bible?

Well, a big deep voice calling out from the dark, "Matthew, this is God; take a message," isn't how we should think of it. Yes, it's true that some of the Bible's human authors sound like they know they are carrying a message from God. The prophets, for example, often begin their speeches, "Thus says the LORD." But others (think of Saint Paul) don't seem aware that they're doing anything more than writing a letter.

We can't say for sure how God chose to act on the individual prophets and evangelists. Maybe God prompted them one way here and a different way there. But in looking at the Bible itself, it seems clear that God doesn't take over people's minds and use them like robots. Check out how Moses bargained with God at the burning bush (see Exodus, chapter 3), how Isaiah stepped forward to give his "Send me!" when he overheard God looking for a spokesman (see Isaiah, chapter 6), or how the angel Gabriel waited for Mary's brave "May it be done to me according to your word" (Luke 1:38). Moses, Isaiah, Mary . . . each of them was somehow a free agent. So even though God is the ultimate author of the Scriptures, each book also has a human author (or authors).* God chose different people to speak God's truth, all the while respecting their own gifts and freedom. And that sounds like good news to me.

---

* A phrase that runs through many official church documents on the Bible is that the Scriptures are "the Word of God in human language."

9 | Do Catholics read the Bible as being word-for-word history?

As completely true? Yes. But as word-for-word history? Not always. Because we believe that God didn't take over the minds of the Bible's human authors, we must pay attention to the writers' intentions and the ways people in their day communicated so that we don't misunderstand their inspired words. They weren't always trying to write history.

Let me give you an example. You are eating lunch in the school commons when you overhear someone complain, "Man . . . the AP chemistry book weighs a ton!" You do not immediately imagine chemistry students in your school driving forklifts to class. Why not? Because you understand that the phrase "weighs a ton" is a purposeful exaggeration: the chemistry book is thick. To take what you just heard as a literal fact would be a mistake (the book weighs two thousand pounds). We know what is meant because we understand that the exaggeration is made to make a point. Words and phrases with such special meanings are called idioms, and every language is full of them. Think of how we use words like *hot, wicked,* and *bad.*

Beyond using idioms, we package our messages to one another in special forms to make understanding easier. If a friend says, "Knock, knock," you know that a joke is coming. If a text begins "Once upon a time," you are expecting an imaginative story. If your parents call you over and say, "Sit down; we need to talk," you know something serious is ahead. The different ways of packaging a message (as a poem, a law code, a parable, a history, an obituary, a love letter, and so on) are called literary forms. To understand a message properly, we need to put it in the literary form the sender used.

In the same way, to receive its message correctly, Catholics read the Bible contextually. Here is how the *Catechism of the Catholic Church* puts it:

> In order to discover *the sacred authors' intention,* the reader must take into account the conditions of their time and culture, the literary genres in use at that time, and the modes of feeling, and narrating then current. "For the fact is that truth is differently presented and expressed in the various types of historical writing, in prophetical and poetical texts, and in other forms of literary expression."[2] (Number 110)

Sometimes the biblical authors mean for us to take their words literally (for example, when Paul describes his experience of the risen Jesus outside Damascus in Galatians, chapter 1). At other spots, God's truth is conveyed by imaginative stories (think of Jesus's parable of the prodigal son in Luke, chapter 15). Reading God's library correctly, then, means learning to receive the text in the way the human authors wanted to be understood. So Catholics don't assume that every Bible statement is historical or scientific. We must always try to understand the Bible in its context. As one of my teachers used to put it: "All of the Bible is true, but only some of it aims to be factual."

10 How can I tell which parts of the Bible are history and which parts are parable or poetry?

It's a matter of learning to recognize the clues. If you receive an 8½-x-11-inch sheet of letterhead with your name and address typed above the greeting "Dear Sir or Madam," you think, "Ah, business letter." But unfold a piece of Precious Moments stationery with "My love, my sweetness, my everything" scrawled at the top with a felt-tip pen, and you know you have something quite different in your hand. You didn't know this automatically. You learned to recognize the form of a business letter in English class, just as you learned the form of a love letter somewhere outside of class.

The challenge when it comes to applying this to God's Word is that the Bible was composed centuries ago. We often need coaching to get the clues. This is where the helps packaged with some Bibles are handy—especially book introductions and footnotes. The multi-paragraph warm-ups at the start of each book prepare you for what to expect—history, poetry, letter, or imaginative story with a moral. Footnotes, usually marked in the text with an asterisk [*] or tiny superscript letter [a], direct you to the small print at the bottom of the page where you will find help with difficult terms or the general meaning of a passage.

11

Can't I understand the Bible on my own?

Though God's Word is addressed to each of us, it comes to us through God's people, the Church. If I read the Bible apart from God's people, I increase my odds of misreading it. Let me serve up an analogy.

Imagine you've been given a large chunk of change to buy a bicycle. You go to your local bike shop and start picking out a frame, tires, derailleurs, and some of those cool biker shorts. You may think you are all set to go, but there's one essential thing the friendly bicycle shop folks can't sell you: the skill to ride the thing. That you must learn. The Bible, like the bike shop, has everything we need in it except the knack of how to understand it.

The larger story of our ancestors' lives of faith, their memory of mistakes and wrong turns, and the way the Holy Spirit has guided them to truth through it all, Catholics call Tradition.* It's God's revealed truth—entrusted to the Church's safekeeping—that helps us live in holiness and grow in faith, handed on not only in the Bible but also in creeds, liturgy, Church statements, and the witness of great souls. Remember what Saint Peter warned—"There is no prophecy of scripture that is a matter of personal interpretation" (2 Peter 1:20)—and save yourself a good deal of confusion and personal weirdness by reading the Scriptures with the Church.

* Note the capital "T." That distinguishes it from the "just how we do it here" customs that change through time (*tradition* with a small "t"). See question 3 in section 3.

12 | Has the Church explained what everything in the Bible means?

Well, no. When some of the disciples asked Jesus, "Where are you staying?" (John 1:38), his answer was not "the third house past the synagogue," but "Come, and you will see" (1:39). The Bible is our invitation to know God in relationship, and can never be boiled down to a Catholic top-ten list or a step-by-step instruction manual for being a Christian. So rather than giving us a list of answers about what the Bible means, the Church hands us a compass and a set of guardrails.

By *compass* I mean that we have available the living memory of how we Catholics have approached and understood God's library through the centuries. This memory comes to us as a set of guiding principles with which to approach the text. In this first section, I've talked about the importance of reading the Bible in context and paying attention to literary forms to introduce you to some of these principles.*

But there isn't much sense in letting travelers head down a dead-end road, is there? So now and again, the Pope and bishops have stepped up to steer Catholics away from certain approaches to God's Word that have proven to be a waste of time or even dangerous. This is what I mean by *guardrails*. They help keep us out of the ditch. In the sixteenth century, for example, these teachers of the Church connected the biblical dots to make clear that Jesus's charge to the disciples, "Whose sins you forgive are forgiven them" (John 20:23), is the foundation for the Sacrament of Penance and Reconciliation. But such official explanations about the meaning of specific biblical texts are actually quite rare.**

So you won't find an official interpretation for every Bible verse on the Vatican Web site. Reading the Bible is more like traveling with Jesus with a few tools in your pocket and keeping a wary eye out for the occasional dead-end roads.

* The most complete treatment of these principles can be found in the Vatican II document *The Dogmatic Constitution on Divine Revelation* (*Dei Verbum*, to give it its Latin title). The most important principles can also be found in a summary form in the *Catechism of the Catholic Church* (see numbers 101–141).

** Check out the footnote for John 20:23 in the New American Bible. For other examples of verses where the Church officially explains the meaning of a Scripture text, see also the notes for Isaiah 7:14 and James 5:15.

13 | Can a Bible passage have more than one meaning?

Absolutely, but the place to start is with what the authors wanted to say. That means paying attention to the clues that help us understand whether God's truth is coming to us in a parable, a poem, or an historical narrative. This is what Catholics call attending to the literal sense of a passage.* If you overlook what the author intended to say, you can end up substituting your own agenda for God's saving truth.

But a Bible passage or story can often point to a truth that goes beyond what the original author understood. This is especially the case when we read the Old Testament with Jesus on our minds. Christians call this "extra meaning" the text's spiritual sense. For example, the promise made to David that his descendants would reign forever (see 2 Samuel 7:12–13) takes on a fresh meaning when we remember Jesus was of David's family. You will find that some Bible stories or passages can have multiple meanings when you explore the spiritual sense.

Even then our work isn't done, for there is also the "So what?" question. To understand a message, I must, at some level, respond to it. My response to a Bible text might mean gaining a new insight about God or myself, choosing a new course of action in my life, or asking further questions. When we open the Bible, there is the author's meaning and possibly an additional spiritual meaning or meanings. So in addition to asking what a Scripture passage means, we must also ask what it means to us.

---

* Warning: Don't confuse this with literalism, which means accepting every line in the Bible as historic or scientific fact. See question 9 in this section.

14 How can I develop a Bible-reading habit?

I don't know if what I have to offer will be new, but let me make some suggestions.

First, check your attitude. I mean come to the Bible at your best—not rushed, not overly tired, not absentmindedly. Treat God's written Word as you would an encounter with a friend. Before you read, pray to God's Holy Spirit to speak to you through these words. Expect to be spoken to.

Next, develop a plan. The Bible is so big and varied, paging around it at random isn't likely to feed your soul. Most people do better with a method. One way is to read a book straight through.* Another way is to read a variety of passages on a common theme.** A third way is to read the Scripture readings that will be read at Mass for today or the coming Sunday's liturgy.*** Pick a method, and then stick to it for a while (like a month or more) before you try something else.

Whatever method you use, don't be afraid to mark in your Bible. If a passage moves you, highlight it or note it with a colored pencil. (Be careful though, as many Bibles are printed on thin paper that ink might bleed through.) This way you can return to a favorite passage more quickly. Or, write down the book, chapter, and verse(s) (called a "citation") on the blank surfaces inside the Bible's front or back covers, along with a word or phrase as to what the passage is about. This way you will begin to build your own list of favorite Bible passages.

As I've said before, use whatever study helps your Bible provides—especially the introductions to the individual books and the explanations you find in the footnotes.

But perhaps the most important thing you need to develop a Bible reading habit is the willingness to pick yourself up when you stumble. The wise teacher knows that "the arrow that hits the bull's-eye is the result of a hundred previous misses." Woe to the people who give up before try number 101, for they shall miss the reward of all their errors.

* See my suggestions in question 1 of this section for good books to start with.

** Another Bible reading tool is a concordance, which is a list of verses that use a particular word. A concordance can help you find passages that speak to a specific theme you want to study. But you have to use the concordance that matches the Bible translation you are using. Alternately, thematic concordances contain lists of biblical passages organized by subject, which can be helpful regardless of the Bible you are using. Actually, some Bibles have a short thematic concordance built right in at the back of the book.

*** If you don't have a bulletin handy but have access to a computer, visit the United States Catholic Conference Web site *(www.usccb.org),* which has a listing of the Bible passages read at Mass for each day of the year.

How can I use the Bible to pray?

Lots of our religious talk is chatter *about* God and religion. But as I've said, because the aim of the Bible isn't just to describe God but to help us have a real friendship with God, it can be a wonderful springboard for developing a conversation with God, with real give and take. Let me introduce you to a simple method of praying the Scriptures that even a beginner can use. It goes by the fancy Latin name *lectio divina*, often translated as "holy reading." Though there are variations on how this kind of prayer is presented, usually there are four steps that (happily) you can easily remember by four "R" words.

Select a Scripture passage for this super slow reading. I'd suggest one of the Gospels or the Book of Psalms as a place to start. After a prayer to the Holy Spirit expressing your desire to meet God here, begin to **read** the passage (out loud, if possible) until some word or phrase moves you or draws your attention. It doesn't matter if your response to the phrase is gratitude, wonder, or recognition; when you have a reaction to some part of the passage, the first step is done.

Then gently **repeat** that word or phrase several times. You aren't trying to puzzle out its meaning but rather to amplify its effect on you by turning it over and over in your mind and heart. If you don't mind a homely image, it's like trying to wring out a wet washcloth, getting the last drop out of the phrase until your heart is full and you feel you want to address God.

So far, this method has put you in the listening mode of prayer. You chose a passage to read, God has touched you with a word, and you have deepened God's word in you by repetition. You have opened yourself up to what God has to say to you. Now **respond.** Simply speak to God (again, I encourage doing this out loud if doing so won't disturb others), expressing how these words touch you, puzzle you, or make you aware of your need. Speak as long as you like.

The fourth step in this prayer form is to **rest.** Be still, letting the words you've heard and the words you've spoken sink in. It's like coasting down a hill after having biked your way to the top. Silence is the language of the Holy Spirit, and in this quiet God will speak a confirming word in your heart.

When you find yourself mentally drawn away or distracted, the resting step is over, and you can pick up the Bible again and continue, repeating the four-step process—read, repeat, respond, rest . . . read, repeat, respond, rest—again and again through your prayer time. The goal isn't to read so many verses but to be in conversation with God for a certain length of time. Some days you may read a whole chapter, other days just a few lines. I wasn't kidding when I said a beginner can do it, but it will serve you well all your life. It's about having a prayerful conversation where God gets to choose the topics.*

* A more detailed explanation of *lectio divina* can be found in *The Catholic Youth Prayer Book*, pages 83–90, also published by Saint Mary's Press (2006).

16

Is there a CliffsNotes version of the whole Bible?

Sure. For all its variety, God's library has a plot—a plot that can be stated in a few sentences. God makes the world and all living things in love. For one reason or another, humankind chooses to reject God. God does not reject us in turn but begins a relentless pursuit of humanity that has continued to right here, right now. If that's a little too thin of a summary, the Bible itself has a couple passages that outline the main story.

Prepping the former Israelite slaves before they cross into the land promised by God, Moses tells them to keep a harvest feast by offering a basket of the earth's good things and reciting this little summary of how they got here:

> My father was a wandering Aramean who went down to Egypt with a small household and lived there as an alien. But there he became a nation great, strong and numerous. When the Egyptians maltreated and oppressed us, imposing hard labor upon us, we cried to the LORD, the God of our fathers, and he heard our cry and saw our affliction, our toil and our oppression. He brought us out of Egypt with his strong hand and outstretched arm, with terrifying power, with signs and wonders; and bringing us into this country, he gave us this land flowing with milk and honey. (Deuteronomy 26:5–9)

God has taken "nobodies" and made them into "somebodies." In a way, that's the whole message of the Old Testament. The first five books of the Bible, the Jewish Torah, are the core of the basic story; the remaining forty-one books of the Old Testament trace the continuing ups and downs of God's relationship with Israel for a thousand years.

But of course the great story didn't end there. When the time was just right, God stepped into time and history in a unique way, taking on our humanness and wearing it so very well, in order to build a bridge from us to God by which we might escape sin and death. Jesus talks about himself and his mission most concisely in the Gospel of John:

> For God so loved the world that he gave his only Son, so that everyone who believes in him might not perish but might have eternal life. For God did not send his Son into the world to condemn the world, but that the world might be saved through him. (John 3:16–17)

There is more to say about Jesus's teaching and mighty works as told in the four Gospels, and about how a handful of his followers grew in numbers and understanding as described in the remaining twenty-three books of the New Testament, but this is the heart of the New Testament story: God is a deliverer.

God has taken "nobodies" and made them into "somebodies." God is a deliverer. You see, the two parts of the Bible are saying the same thing. Perhaps you better understand now what I said at the opening of this section: something like this really could change your life.

Section 2: FAQs on Tough Texts in the Bible

Maybe you have heard what is supposedly Mark Twain's quip about the Scriptures: "It ain't those parts of the Bible I don't understand that bother me, so much as the parts that I do understand." There is a whole lot of truth there. All the same, there are more than a few passages in God's Word that can seem mystifying. How do you square the Genesis story of Creation with Darwin's theory of evolution? Why does the Old Testament God seems so violent? What's the deal with the number 666 in the Book of Revelation? If you have looked at the questions in the first section of this book, you may feel more settled about the structure of the Bible, but now we have to face some of the stuff inside.

In this section, we are going to look at some "tough texts"—Scripture passages that end up getting a lot of attention. "Follow the weird," one of my seminary professors would say, "because where the Bible is most challenging is exactly where you are most likely to discover something new about our God." That is the point of all this work, of course: to prepare ourselves to meet the living God.

The twenty-three questions and answers here are organized in the order that the passages in question appear in the Bible, from Genesis to Revelation. Though each question addresses a different Scripture passage and is independent of the other "tough text" questions, my responses often rely on distinctions introduced in section 1, so be prepared to look back now and again. Along the way, you will meet passages from almost every "shelf" in God's library. Here's hoping that by the end of this section, following the weird doesn't seem too weird after all!

1 Does taking the Bible seriously mean I have to believe that the world was created in six days (see Genesis 1:1—2:4a)?

Not at all. For some people, "taking the Bible seriously" means "taking its every statement as a scientific or historical fact," but that isn't the case for Catholics. In section 1, I made the point that for us recognizing a text's literary form is key to getting the author's point.* An obituary, a knock-knock joke, and a parking ticket are all different literary forms with different purposes, and telling the three apart can help us from embarrassing ourselves. If the communicator is standing right there (or is a phone call away) and we're unclear about the message, we can always check by asking for a clarification. This isn't possible with the human authors of the Bible, of course, but they have left us clues.

With Genesis, chapters 1–2, we should start by asking, "What kind of writing is this?" A quick read might suggest the Bible's opening chapters mean to explain how the universe came to be. To a twenty-first-century American, that sounds like a scientific claim, but we shouldn't automatically assume that's how an Israelite thirty centuries ago would have understood it. Most cultures across the globe have their own stories about how the world came to be. If you read the first chapters of Genesis carefully, you will find that even our Bible has two distinct Creation accounts.** How can we explain all this variety? A first reaction might be to assume that the Genesis stories are somehow historical, and every other culture's creation story is just made up. But a better tack would be to ask ourselves, "What is it exactly that Creation stories try to do?" As a specific type of literature, their purpose isn't to give scientific explanations.

We are fascinated with the science behind how the universe and life came to be, but it seems most ancient peoples, including the Hebrews, were more into asking why and for what purpose we came to be. As Pope John Paul II put it, the Bible "does not wish to teach how heaven was made but how one goes to heaven."*** Taking the Bible seriously demands that we read it as its authors intended, and scientific explanations were not usually their aim. Though the Church hasn't defined the literal meaning of Genesis, chapters 1–2, recent Church statements presuppose an ancient universe, slowly shaped through time. There is no necessary conflict between our Catholic faith and the findings of science.

* See section 1, question 9.

** Notice that in Genesis 1:1–2:4a (the first story), God calls the created world out of chaotic waters on day 1, birds and fish are a product of day 5, and humans and other land creatures come along on day 6. In Genesis 2:4b–25 (the second story), the Lord God first shapes a human being out of clay, then plants a garden in an apparently desert landscape, and only then creates birds, fish, and other living beings.

*** "John Paul II: Scripture and Science: The Path of Scientific Discovery," in *Origins*, 1981, page 279. The Pope was playing with a statement of the sixteenth-century astronomer Galileo, who was quoting the fifth-century bishop Saint Augustine.

2

If the Creation stories in the Bible (see Genesis 1:1—2:4a, 2:4b–24) are not scientific explanations of creation, what are they trying to say?

The Bible's Creation stories are concerned less with the details of how the universe was constructed and more with the saving truth about God, us, and God-and-us. Our ancestors in faith had a unique perspective on the nature of God. This becomes clearer if you compare the Genesis accounts of Creation with one of the other creation stories that floated around at the same time. The ancient Babylonian story of creation, for example, opens with a family feud among the many gods, which leads to a grand battle. The winning deity then shapes the universe from the corpse of his defeated rival, and mixes earth with the blood of one of his slain captains to fashion human beings. Hmm . . . tasty. Now how would such a story prepare you for growing up Babylonian? To me it sounds like the universe was an afterthought, life is a violent struggle, and that we human beings have the stuff of the rebel in us. That's one way of looking at life, but it's not the biblical way.

In Genesis there is no heavenly rivalry or battle, and no question about who's in charge. In the first Creation story (see Genesis 1:1–2:4a), the universe comes into being as God puts order to chaos by sheer command and then populates the new spaces with stars and the sun and plants and living beings. A close look reveals that each day's retelling has the same orderly structure ("Then God said: 'Let there be . . .' and so it happened . . . evening came, and morning followed—the fill-in-the-blank day"). Several days end with a refrain: "And God saw how good it was." And on the sixth working day, God creates humans "in his image" (Genesis 1:27) as the pinnacle of his efforts, blesses all living things, and charges the woman and man with a special responsibility over the rest. Sometimes the universe doesn't look very tidy, and sometimes life doesn't feel very good, but despite that, the first Hebrew Creation story boldly proclaims (1) God made the universe, (2) made it on purpose, (3) made it good, and (4) gave human beings a special bearing and role in it.

The second Creation story (see Genesis 2:4b–24) offers another perspective on the nature of God and a little added insight about us. Unlike the commanding creative presence of Genesis, chapter 1, here God is more the artist, scooping up clay, shaping the human creature, poking holes for eyes and ears (well, I added that part), and breathing in God's very own life. The story continues with the Creator's providing a partner for the man—not from clay, like the other animals—but from the first human's own side.

So which is it? Is God distant and powerful and transcendent (as suggested in Genesis, chapter 1), or is God close and involved and intimate (as Genesis, chapter 2, tells it)? "Well," say the Creation stories of the Bible, "God is both."

3 | Were Adam and Eve real people (see Genesis 3:1–24)?

I would say they *represent* real people. Let me explain. There's a fifteenth-century play where a fellow, about to die, tries to recruit aspects of his life to stand with him as he is judged by God. Beauty, Possessions, and his Relatives all beg off. Only Good Deeds (the personification of the man's generosity) agrees to come along. The drama is really about all of us, is all of us, and is appropriately named *Everyman*.

The Hebrew name Adam means "human being," and Genesis 3:20 connects the name Eve with the word for "life," so the names of the first pair invite us from the start to see them as the biblical "Everyman / Everywoman." When our kind appeared on earth,* from the beginning they turned away from God and in upon themselves. So the story of the Fall from God's grace in Genesis, chapter 3, uses "figurative language" (*Catechism of the Catholic Church*, number 390) to teach that human history has always been marked by the tragic and self-inflicted rejection of God's gifts, beginning with our first parents. This inherited distance from God and others, which we call Original Sin, is very real.

* Catholics are free to hold that human beings developed from other life forms through a process of natural selection (see Darwin's Theory of Evolution) so long as they recognize that there is a uniquely God-given component as well, our souls. For more on that, check Pope John Paul II's address to the Pontifical Academy of Sciences, "Truth Cannot Contradict Truth" (October 22, 1996).

4

What am I supposed to get out of the long lists of ancestors (the genealogies) in the Bible (see Genesis 4:17–22, 5:1–32, chapter 10, 11:10–32)?

If "who you know" is important in our culture, "who you are related to" mattered even more in the biblical world. The names of your parents, grandparents, and great-grandparents might decide whom you could marry, what jobs you were eligible for, and how well (or badly) others would treat you. Lists of ancestors and descendants were very important then: it was thought they explained who you were.

The Bible genealogies contain other meanings as well. Consider the family tree from Adam to Abraham in Genesis 5:1–32 and 11:10–32. In these lists, each generation's life grows shorter—from Adam's astronomic 930 years to Terah's (Abraham's father) reduced, if still generous, 210 years. Some folks come up with elaborate explanations to explain how people could live so very long back then, but again, it's likely that the author's intention here is more symbolic than historical. If you scan the whole genealogy, you'll see the length of the patriarchs' lives grows shorter just as the surrounding stories (the Fall, Cain and Abel, Noah and the Flood, the Tower of Babel) catalog how human rebellion increases. Besides linking the stories together, the genealogies make the point that as sin increases, life diminishes. Though these ancestor lists may not make exciting reading, don't skip them. They too are part of the inspired story.

5

What does it mean when God tells Moses his name is "I AM WHO I AM" (see Exodus 3:4–14)?

It may come as a surprise to you, but "God" is not originally a name. In the world where the ancient Jews lived, every nation had its own team of gods and goddesses, each with his or her own personal name. Baal was the Canaanite god of the storm, Demeter the Greek goddess of agriculture, and so on. "God" is the category to which they all belong; calling out the name Baal or Demeter was how you got a specific god or goddess's attention.

So when a voice from the burning bush calls to Moses and claims to be the god of his ancestors, Moses has good reason to ask, "But just who are you?" The response he receives, "I AM WHO I AM" (Exodus 3:14, NRSV), doesn't seem to say too much at first, but "I am" is the idea behind the special name by which the Israelites came to know their one and only god: Yahweh. The name is rich with meanings. You should hear in it a reference to God's creative role ("I cause to be what is"), a promise ("I will be with you"), and a statement of mystery ("I am beyond you"). Don't be frustrated by the fact that it might mean more than one thing. Remember, God is big.

Over time the Jewish people came to believe that using God's personal name was a little too casual. Long before Jesus, they began using the title "my Lord" in place of God's personal name. Most English Bibles respect that practice, printing LORD (in small caps) throughout the Old Testament where the name Yahweh appears in the original.

6 **When Moses asked Pharoah to release the Hebrew slaves, the Bible says, "the LORD hardened the heart of Pharoah" (Exodus 9:12, NRSV). So isn't it unfair that God turns around and punishes the Egyptians with plagues?**

You've put your finger on a real puzzler. In the struggle with Pharaoh (Egypt's king), Yahweh appears to be making Pharaoh stubborn (see Exodus 7:3; 10:1,20,27; 11:10; 14:4,8,17). But in the same chapters, we're told that the king hardened his own heart (see Exodus 7:13,14,22; 8:11,15,28; 9:7,34,45). This sort of thing pops up all through the Bible: on the one hand, God is almighty, all knowing, and controls everything. On the other hand, human beings aren't puppets; our choices are important. For example, the psalmist marvels that God is aware of our words before we utter them: "Even before a word is on my tongue, LORD, you know it all" (Psalm 139:4). But another biblical voice emphasizes that our decisions matter: "When God . . . created man, he made him subject to his own free choice. / If you choose you can keep / the commandments" (Sirach 15:14–15a).

Sometimes to explain something really big, we resort to using seeming opposites. Light is a wave, but it is also a particle. A mother's love is gentle, but it is also fierce. The truth of things is often bigger than any one statement alone. So it is when we ask who is in charge of our lives. Any explanation we give must say two things: (1) nothing happens without God's knowing and permitting it, and (2) our free will is one of God's best gifts to us. This was true for Pharaoh, and it is true for us.

Why did God tell the Israelites to wipe out all the people, including women and children, who were living in the Promised Land (see Deuteronomy 7:1–11, 20:10–18)?

The Books of Deuteronomy and Joshua tell of the early steps in the relationship between the Israelites and Yahweh, their deliverer. The way the story runs, God's People were to have a clean start in a new land, and anything (or anyone) that would sway them to return to their old ways had to be eliminated. It may not be altogether different from how our parents suggest we stay away from certain individuals who could be bad influences on us.

But behind this question lies a bigger concern: "How could God, who told us, 'Thou shall not kill,' and whose Son told us 'to love our enemies,' command the destruction of innocent people?" If you read questions 1 and 2 in section 1, you will remember how we talked about the Bible's being a collection of writings written by many God-inspired human hands. An important principle that comes from that idea is to let one part of God's library help inform our understanding of another part. The human authors grew in their understanding of God through time.

Maybe another example will help. It may come as a surprise, but for most of the Old Testament period, the Jewish people didn't seem to have a crystal clear expectation of life after death.* But by Jesus's day, some Jews—including Jesus himself, of course—had come to see that God's plan for us (like God's love) is forever.** It took a while, but the Israelites came to a fuller idea about God's plan for them, now including the possibility of resurrection. One part of the Bible balances and develops another.

So back to your original question. The Old Testament command to root out Israel's enemies in the Promised Land comes at an early stage in the whole story. At the time, the Israelites believed that God wanted them, in order to stay pure, to wipe out people who didn't believe like them. In the New Testament, Jesus corrects and supplements some earlier beliefs—like this one—about what God really wants. For example, he quotes a law given to Moses only to break it apart: "You have heard that it was said, 'An eye for an eye and a tooth for a tooth.' But I say to you, offer no resistance to one who is evil. When someone strikes you on [your] right cheek, turn the other one to him as well" (Matthew 5:38–39). So Jesus presents a picture of God's will that at times seems different from that presented in the opening books of the Bible. Those differences do not mean that God has changed, but rather that our understanding of God needed further growth. That's why we ought to be wary of grabbing onto one verse and saying, "See, here is what the Bible says about X." We need to read one part of the Scriptures with all the other parts of God's library in mind.

* Check out Psalm 6:6 or Sirach 10:10–11 for a description of the "blah existence" most Jews evidently thought awaited us all.

** See Wisdom 3:1–9, Daniel 12:1–3, and Mark 12:18–27.

Why don't we follow all the laws Moses gave the Israelites (see Exodus 20:1— 23:33 and Leviticus 11:1—27:34)?

As a rule, Americans aren't big on rules. We tend to think the fewer of them, the better. The Israelites, on the other hand, though not into regulations for their own sake, got pretty excited about the laws that Moses presented them as gifts from Yahweh. "The law of the Lord is perfect, / refreshing the soul," sings the psalmist (Psalm 19:8). The newly freed slaves were so pleased about God's Law because they saw it as an entrance into the mind and heart of their Deliverer. "Surely," they reasoned, "knowing the heart and mind of God will lead to life!"

Many of the laws revealed in the Books of Exodus, Leviticus, Numbers, and Deuteronomy are ethical in nature. They address how to treat one another (think, "Thou shalt not kill, steal, bear false witness, and so on") and are the part of the Israelite law most familiar to Christians. But other Old Testament laws aim at organizing the Israelites' ritual life. These showed the Israelites how to honor God in their worship life and diet by respecting the lines drawn in Creation between what they believed to be "clean" and "unclean" things. So there are certain ways to make an offering in the Temple, special seasons to be observed, and certain foods to be avoided. It's not a perfect image, but think of the ethical laws as the horizontal dimension of the Law (obligations to others and to creation) and ritual laws as the vertical dimension of the Law (pointers to our relationship with God).

Jesus had the greatest regard for the Old Testament's ethical laws, even clarifying and amplifying them at times. For example, he famously expanded the Sixth Commandment, the one against adultery, to include lustful thoughts (see Matthew 5:27–28) and raised the bar on how many times we must forgive those who wrong us (see Matthew 18:21–22). But where the ritual laws came in, Jesus was more flexible—frequently crossing the boundaries other religious teachers worried about. Despite the regulations in Leviticus, chapter 14, Jesus touched a leper (see Mark 1:41–51). He showed a more relaxed understanding of the Sabbath rest command in Exodus 34:21 when he defended his disciples' casual Sabbath-day harvesting (see Mark 2:23–28). He ate with the sorts of people the Law, and your mother, warned you about (see Mark 2:13–17, Luke 15:1–2). Like many of the best teachers in Judaism before him, he got frustrated when people settled for "going through the motions" of religion, while they excused themselves from honoring God and creation in truth and action.

By the Holy Spirit's prompting, the first Christians came to see that many of the Jewish ritual laws had become an obstacle to preaching the good news of God's saving work. At the Council of Jerusalem, the Apostles agreed not to ask Jesus's non-Jewish followers to bother with more than a handful of the ritual laws (see Acts of the Apostles 15:6–29). So, although Jesus's words confirmed (and sometimes expanded) the ethical demands of the Mosaic Law, Christians are not obligated to follow the Jewish rules governing diet, association, and worship.

Why is there so much violence against women in the Book of Judges?

Throughout biblical times, Israelite society was a place where most important decisions were in the hands of men. Though women occasionally play leading roles in the narrative (check out the stories of Eve, Sarah, Miriam, Deborah, Esther, and Ruth for starters*), the Bible mainly leaves women unnamed and unnoted. Unfortunately, the evidence we have is clear that men were dominant in the culture of the ancient Near East. The first thing to understand when reading accounts of women being treated badly in the Bible—or being overlooked altogether—is that the Mediterranean world was slanted in favor of adult men.

Even admitting that, few Bible readers are prepared for the way women are treated in the portion of Israel's story that details life after reaching the Promised Land. With the exception of the prophetess and judge, Deborah, and the mighty heroine, Jael (see Judges, chapters 4–5), when women surface at all in the Book of Judges, they are being sacrificed as payment for a father's rash vow (see Judges, chapter 11), pushed forward for abuse in place of men (see Judges 19:22–28), and kidnapped and forced into marriage (see Judges, chapter 21).

The thing to remember here is that just because a statement or action appears in the Bible, we shouldn't assume it's there for our imitation. Indeed the bad news in the Scriptures is often there to demonstrate a need for God's good news. Do you remember how, right after declaring the goodness of Creation, Genesis featured a little landslide of stories signaling the spread of humanity's rebellion against God?** Something like that is happening in the Book of Judges. The treatment of women and children and foreigners—those the ancient world viewed as most vulnerable—served as a kind of biblical barometer for the godliness of the community (see Exodus 22:20–23). So the increasing level of violence of men against women and among the Israelite tribes in the Book of Judges is heralding that God's people are reaching another critical point. This is underscored by a repeated refrain in the book's latter chapters as the explanation for the mess: "In those days there was no king in Israel; everyone did what he thought best" (Judges 17:6, 21:25; see 18:1, 19:1). Something was going wrong, says the inspired author, and as the continuation of the story in the Books of Samuel will tell, the people would ask for a remedy in the form of a king.

Judges is for many a disturbing book. We read it at times not to find something to imitate, but something we need to guard against.

* Read about Eve in Genesis, chapters 2–3; Sarah in Genesis, chapters 12, 16–18, 21, 23; Miriam in Exodus, chapter 15, Numbers, chapters 12 and 20, and Micah 6:4; Deborah in Judges, chapters 4–5. Esther and Ruth are the main characters in complete books that bear their names.

** See this mentioned in question 4 of this section.

10

In some of the psalms, the writers call down curses on their enemies (see Psalms 58, 83, 109). How can a prayer like that be in the Bible?

I remember once hearing a talk on the Psalms advertised as "Prayers for When You're Sad, Glad, or Mad." Indeed the Old Testament's Book of Psalms has poems for just about every human mood and teaches us how we might address God in every situation. It can be a jolt when cruising through a particularly lovely psalm-prayer, like Psalm 139, to run across lines like: "If only you would destroy the wicked, O God . . . / Do I not hate, LORD, those who hate you? . . . / With fierce hatred I hate them, / enemies I count as my own" (Psalm 139:19a, 21a–22). Scholars call such statements curses or imprecations, and plenty of them can be found in the Book of Psalms and throughout the Bible.*

These evil wishes embarrass many Christians. After all, wasn't Jesus clear that his disciples ought to "love your enemies, do good to those who hate you, . . . pray for those who abuse you" (Luke 6:27b–28, NRSV)? Sensitive people ask, "Can't we cut these verses out of the Bible or at least skip them when we pray?" As understandable as such a move might be at first, the suggestion forgets that God is the author of every part of God's library.

Jesus certainly prayed these Psalms as a faithful Jew. So how might he have prayed them? Though there were certainly those who opposed him, Jesus knew his real enemy was not a particular scribe or sinner, but the Devil himself, the father of evil, whose offspring are hate, violence, sickness, and death. These Jesus opposed, even though he showed the utmost concern for the people in whom they lodged. When Jesus prayed these psalms, he was probably thinking that these are the things to be cursed rather than the specific people.**

We too can pray these psalms if we direct our prayerful anger not at specific people, but at the things and attitudes that seem to thwart God's intentions for us. One of my parishioners explained to me how he aimed the words of the cursing psalms against his wife's out-of-control cancer cells—expressing both his anger and his prayer for God's healing presence to defeat and destroy this enemy. And when in my own prayer I come across the last line of Psalm 137—"Happy those who seize your children / and smash them against a rock."—I don't think of the Babylonian babies the original author probably had in mind; rather, I think of sin's children in me: selfishness, pride, and deceit. These things in me need to be destroyed. And the one to do them in, of course, is Jesus.

* For a sampling, check out Psalms 21:9–13; 31:18–19; 54:7; 59:6–9,12–16; 69:23–29, and 143:12. Psalms 58, 83, and 109 are almost all curses.

** This is an example of looking for the "spiritual sense" in Scripture that I mention in question 13 of section 1.

What's fear of the Lord (see Psalm 34:9), and why does the Bible think I should want it?

The Bible is very high on the fear of the Lord. We're told to "serve the LORD with fear" (Psalm 2:11) and that fear of the Lord "is the beginning of knowledge" (Proverbs 1:7). We read that fear of the Lord is a spiritual gift possessed by the awaited Messiah (see Isaiah 11:2).* Yet over and over again in God's library, the Israelites and the disciples are told to not be afraid. So which is it? Is being afraid of God a good thing or a bad thing?

Like the word *pine* in *pineapple, fear* takes on a new meaning when combined with the phrase "of the Lord." Instead of meaning "panic" or "anxiety," it means "showing proper respect for God's holiness and greatness." Fear of the Lord embraces all the parts of a relationship with God. The difference between the bad fear we should avoid and the good fear we should cultivate is demonstrated best in the Bible at Exodus 20:20, where Moses tells the Hebrews, in the same breath, "Do not be afraid, for God has come to you only to test you and put his fear upon you, lest you should sin." The second reference to fear ("put his fear upon you") is the fear of the Lord. It's a good thing.

* The seven gifts of the Holy Spirit associated with the Sacrament of Confirmation come from this list of the Messiah's attributes in the Book of Isaiah.

12 What's with all the steamy talk in the Song of Songs?

If you have yet to take the plastic wrap off your Bible, you could be in for a surprise. The Song of Songs is just what it appears to be—a collection of passionate love poems shared between a young woman and young man. It starts right at the beginning with "Let him kiss me with kisses of his mouth!" (1:2). And I didn't add the exclamation point—it's in the translation.

The book is like a play, with lines for the girl, her female friends, and the boy. To help the reader follow the ups and downs of their relationship, some translations even print cues for the speakers in the margin. Personal highlights for many are the occasional poetic descriptions of one by the other, comparing parts of their anatomy to features of life and nature (see 4:1–7, 5:10–16, 7:2–6). These can seem wildly funny at times ("Your hair is like a flock of goats / streaming down the mountains" [4:1b]), but it's obvious each of them has been thinking about the other a lot.

But what is this doing in God's library? At one level, the presence of the Song of Songs in the Bible is a celebration of human love as a gift from God. But in a second flash of inspiration, an anonymous Jewish sage saw in these breathless "I can't get you off my mind" sentiments a picture of God's extravagant love for us and a model for a properly ardent response on our part. The steamy talk in the Song of Songs, then, is pretty important stuff—about the best of human love and about our relationship with God.

13 Did a whale really swallow the prophet Jonah (see Jonah 2:1,11)?

To be able to answer that question absolutely, of course, I'd have had to have been there. The next best thing would be to phone the author to find out what she or he intended. But, of course, that isn't a real alternative either. Our next best option, then, is to try to assess just what sort of writing, what literary form, the story of Jonah is, based on the clues within the text. Good writers give us such hints, and this author is a great writer. Based on the clues we find in the Book of Jonah itself, we can say this piece of God's library is a prophetic parable, a story with a meaning. And, as with the parables of Jesus, the historical details aren't the point.

What are these clues? Well, about everything in the book is the opposite of what we would expect. First, the Book of Jonah is different from the rest of the prophetic writings in form. Isaiah, Micah, and the others are chiefly God's words spoken through the prophet (poetry), but Jonah is a story about the prophet (a narrative). Unlike the other prophets who mainly addressed the Jews, Jonah's mission was to reach the non-Jewish Ninevites. If you read carefully, you will notice that although all the non-Jewish characters are noble, faithful, and responsive to Yahweh, the Jewish Jonah bucks God from first verse to last. Feeling unqualified for the role was a common theme for God's messengers, but Jonah takes that to extremes by heading west when Yahweh wants him to go east. And though resistance to a prophet's message is proverbial, this prophet is astoundingly successful: the king of Nineveh, the people, and even the animals repent! Finally, Jonah reacts to his success on God's behalf by being very, very crabby about it.

It's as if Jonah is the flip side of what a prophet should be! And I think that's the point. A flaw in us religious people is the tendency to automatically associate our opinions and judgments with God's opinions and judgments. Jonah is a poster child for our tendency to be smug and superior about our faith, and his story is a warning not to limit God's generosity. The Book of Jonah would have us laugh at ourselves in a wonderful parable of God's mercy.*

And what part does the whale play in this? Well, a very small one. The book doesn't even mention a whale. The "great fish" is just the delivery system God uses to return the runaway prophet to his starting point so God can give Jonah a second try. I don't doubt for a minute that, if need be, God could use a sea creature to give an unwilling messenger a ride, but to get caught up in whether and how it happened is really to miss the point of the story altogether.

* I confess to borrowing most of that phrase (everything but *wonderful*) from the introduction to the Book of Jonah in the New American Bible, the Bible translation owned by the United States Conference of Catholic Bishops. You can see how choosing a Bible with helpful tools for Catholics can help you read the Bible "with the Church."

14 Could the biblical prophets see the future?

In general conversation, people think of biblical prophets as something like fortune tellers. Actually, we'd do better to think of them as physicians. Imagine I go to my local clinic for a check-up. After the doctor probes and prods, he announces, "Father Pierce, if you don't change your diet and exercise habits, I see a heart attack ahead of you." Can the doctor see the future? No, but he is a very informed observer of the signs at hand. Noting my cholesterol level, my blood pressure, and my family health history, he can make a rather informed guess as to where my nightly quart of ice cream is leading me.

The biblical prophets had a clear vision that Yahweh wanted only righteousness and well-being for his people. They knew that living in relationship with God and in accord with the Law would lead them there. On the other hand, they also knew that living apart from God and the Law was bound to leave them empty and unhappy. No more than a doctor wants to see a patient have a heart attack did God's messengers desire that their warnings be confirmed in the people's actual destruction.* Their refrain was always, "Listen, that you may have life" (Isaiah 55:3a). So trade in your picture of Isaiah or Amos standing before a crystal ball. Better you imagine them with a white coat and stethoscope looking for signs of disease in their community. Prophets, then, are not so much fortune tellers as physicians.

* Jonah is the exception here. See question 13 in this section.

15

If Isaiah and Micah predicted his coming, how is it that the Jewish people were so slow to understand that Jesus was the Messiah (see Isaiah 7:10–14, 52:13—53:10; Micah 5:1–4a)?

Have you heard the phrase "hindsight is 20/20"? Looking back after something big has happened, we can often see signs and hints of what was coming . . . but only after the fact.

The Old Testament prophets announced at various times that Yahweh intended prosperity and peace for humanity (see Micah 4:1–5), that he would raise up a new ruler from David's line to bring about justice (see Jeremiah 23:1–6), and that he would even use the suffering of his servants to bring healing to the people (see Isaiah 52:13—53:12). But how these intentions would be worked out wasn't obvious until a surprising and remarkable act of God provided the necessary key: Jesus's death and Resurrection.

Even the original disciples needed more than a little help to understand what Saint Paul called "the mystery hidden for ages in God" (Ephesians 3:9). You can see it happening for two of Jesus's followers in his appearance to them on the road to Emmaus (see Luke 24:13–35). Cleopas and his nameless companion are heading out of Jerusalem early on the Sunday after Jesus's death. They are heartbroken and confused. They evidently had traveled to the city among Jesus's larger band of followers expecting great things, and now they are returning home. Even news that some of their number had found the Master's tomb empty will not keep them in town. When a stranger joins them on their way, they do not recognize him. Then the stranger opens up to them the meaning hidden in the prophetical visions:

And he said to them, "Oh, how foolish you are! How slow of heart to believe all that the prophets spoke!" . . . Then beginning with Moses and all the prophets, he interpreted to them what referred to him in all the scriptures. (Luke 24:25,27)

The bulb finally goes on for them when this stranger takes bread for the evening meal and blesses it. Only then "their eyes were opened" (24:31) and they recognized the resurrected Jesus.

We should be careful about judging Jesus's contemporaries for not automatically seeing him as the fulfillment to the prophets' age-old visions. From the outset, these things were better understood looking back than looking forward.

16 How do you explain the differences in the four Gospels?

Most of us get our initial picture of Jesus from Bible stories our families tell us and from the readings we hear at Mass. These images and sayings get blended in our brain to form a "homogenized" Jesus. Though I actually have met a few people who like to mash all their food together before they eat it, most of us prefer to let the individual flavors speak. If the blended Jesus is the only one you know, you are in for a treat when you meet the four separate portraits of Jesus preserved by Mark, Matthew, Luke, and John.

I speak of four portraits, but it's the same Jesus, of course. Ask my sister, my two brothers, and me about our dad, and you will get wildly different impressions of him, because the same person can look different to the oldest son, the only girl, the spoiled youngest, and the well-balanced normal child (that's me). Jesus's healing ministry and sacrificial death is what impressed Mark most. Matthew added to that picture an emphasis on Jesus as teacher. Luke knew about Christ's saving work and his teaching, but he presented additional snapshots of Jesus's compassion to sinners and outcasts and women. With John's Gospel, it's as if we've been given X-ray glasses to look beneath the surface to see in clearest truth that Jesus is God's very self come among us.

When you open the Gospels and meet the four faces of Jesus, you will notice not only different incidents in his life but also differences in how the authors tell the same incidents. Matthew, for example, has a longer version of the Lord's Prayer than Luke (compare Matthew 6:9–13 with Luke 11:2–4). Jesus cleanses the Temple right at the start in John (see 2:13–25), but the other three place that event in the last week of Jesus's life (see Mark 11:15–19).

The presence of these many little differences is explained by looking at how the stories of Jesus were passed on. The Apostles didn't each go to their own rooms on Easter night and write their memoirs. In a world where maybe 10 percent of the population at best could read, that wouldn't have been a very effective way to get the word out. Instead the Acts of the Apostles tell us they went off and preached about Jesus; only along the way did things get written down. Because the stories circulated separately, it's no surprise the evangelists at times gathered and set them down in differing orders.

The *Catechism of the Catholic Church* handily summarizes the three-stage process that produced the Gospels (see paragraphs 125–127): first, what Jesus really said and did; second, what the Apostles preached after having come to understand more fully these events in the wake of Easter; and, third, what the evangelists selected, and sometimes synthesized, from what they had received orally and in writing, putting on papyrus the truth about Jesus. The four Gospels, with all their differences, give a fuller portrait of the one saving Lord than any one of them could give by itself.

17

Did Jesus have brothers and sisters (see Mark 6:1–3)?

That's actually a question the Bible, by itself, doesn't answer. The New Testament evidence can be read in different ways.

There are places where reference is made to Jesus's brothers and sisters. When he returns to preach at Nazareth, for example, the hometown crowd remarks: "Is he not the carpenter, the son of Mary, and the brother of James and Joses and Judas and Simon? And are not his sisters here with us?" (Mark 6:3). Mark 3:32, John 7:5, Acts of the Apostles 1:14, and 1 Corinthians 9:5 all make references to Jesus's brothers.

But it's not automatically clear just who these people are in relation to Jesus. Though English has precise terms to distinguish siblings, half-brothers and half-sisters, stepbrothers and stepsisters, cousins, nieces, and the like, Hebrew and Aramaic (the languages spoken by Jesus and his disciples) tend to use the same words, *brother ('ach)* and *sister ('ahot),* for all these relationships. So when speaking of Jesus's brothers and sisters, the evangelist Mark could have been referring to cousins rather than Jesus's actual siblings.

Eastern Orthodox Christians understand the brothers and sisters of Jesus mentioned in the Gospels as children of Joseph from a previous marriage; Catholics, using the broader biblical use of *brother,* take them to be Jesus's cousins. This is one of those places where the Bible, by itself, doesn't fully answer a question. It's a reminder to us that the Gospels are more than biographies.

18 Does the Bible say anything about Jesus's being married?

Despite all the excitement surrounding *The DaVinci Code* and its various spin-offs, there is no evidence that Jesus was married. The arguments that Jesus had a wife aren't based on any data about Jesus himself, but on assumptions about normal behavior in Jesus's day.

For example, the first-century Jewish people saw marriage and the bearing of children as a way of honoring God's command to "be fruitful and multiply" (Genesis 1:28, NRSV). So, the reasoning goes, because nothing in the Gospels specifically says Jesus wasn't married, shouldn't we assume that as a faithful Jew he was married? This is called an argument from silence, and it collapses on itself rather quickly.

How about if I can find an example of some very religious Jews who chose not to marry? Well, I can provide three: centuries before Jesus, the prophet Jeremiah remained unmarried at God's request (see Jeremiah 16:1–4); at the same time that Jesus lived, the Essenes, a community of religious Jews, encouraged its members to remain unmarried; and then there's Saint Paul (see 1 Corinthians 7:7–8).

By the way, though Jesus otherwise shows himself very high on family and children, he does in fact give a reason for why someone might choose to forgo marriage for God when he speaks of those who "have renounced marriage for the sake of the kingdom" (Matthew 19:12). That description would seem to fit him perfectly. In any case, there is no evidence anywhere that Jesus was married.

19

Whatever did Jesus mean when he talked about the need for "hating [your] father and mother, wife and children, brothers and sisters" (Luke 14:26) as the price of following him?

Something in Jesus's remark about hating those closest to us rubs us the wrong way. After all, Jesus summed up the whole Law as loving God with all our heart and our neighbor as ourselves (see Mark 12:33). He told us not to hate our enemies but to love them (see Matthew 5:43–47). We even have a Gospel snapshot of Jesus's obeying his parents as a child (see Luke 2:51). In the face of all this, one must suspect that Jesus was either having a bad day when he spoke about "hating father and mother" or that his words are to be taken in more than a literal sense.

The evidence suggests that Jesus was overstating his point for emphasis. It's what we're doing when we say something cost us an arm and a leg. It's called hyperbole, and we understand Jesus to be using hyperbole when he tells his followers to cut off their hands or pluck out their eyes if they are leading them to sin (see Mark 9:43–48).

Jesus wants us to keep the most important things most important. Though my mother, my Xbox, my pet goldfish, and God are all important to me, they probably shouldn't all be equally important. So Jesus looks his disciples square in the face and demands that our relationship with him come first. It's that important. This understanding of what "hating father and mother" means is confirmed in the way Matthew records the same teaching: "Whoever loves father or mother more than me is not worthy of me" (Matthew 10:37). If Matthew's version says it clearer, Luke's version—by exaggeration—at least grabs your attention.

20) What did Jesus mean when he said "the poor you will always have with you" (Matthew 26:11, Mark 14:7; see John 12:8)?

This is an example of what I call an un-Jesus-like saying—that is, words of Jesus that don't match our image of what we think he should say. Putting his words back into their context in the Gospel will help.

Jesus drops this line during a dinner in the last week of his life. In Mark's version, a nameless woman has poured a flask of expensive ointment over Jesus's head, causing others in the room to grumble about this seeming waste in the face of the needs of the poor. That's when Jesus speaks:

> Let her alone. . . . She has done a good thing for me. The poor you will always have with you, and whenever you wish you can do good to them, but you will not always have me. She has done what she could. She has anticipated anointing my body for burial. (Mark 14:6–8)

The first thing to notice is that Jesus isn't mainly talking about the poor here; he is talking about himself. In a few days, he will be dead. In spite of his triple announcement of his fate earlier, no one around him seems to have a clue except this woman. I think Mark wants us to see her extravagant action as the proper response to her Master's impending extravagant gift of himself.

More important, when Jesus says "you always have the poor with you,"* he is actually quoting the first part of a verse from Deuteronomy. In legislating the forgiving of debts every seventh (Sabbath) year, Moses said:

If one of your kinsmen in any community is in need . . . you shall not harden your heart nor close your hand to him in his need. . . . The needy will never be lacking in the land; that is why I command you to open your hand to your poor and needy kinsman. (Deuteronomy 15:7,11)

Moses mentions the poor not to make a prediction, but to prompt the Hebrews to act generously. "There are poor; be ready to respond to them." Just as we could hope today that an intelligent audience could complete a familiar saying when we cite the first part ("Knock, knock" or "Give me liberty"), so Jesus was, I think, counting on the audience to finish "you always have the poor with you" with "open your hand to the poor and needy neighbor in the land." Far from being an excuse for neglecting the poor, then, Jesus's response to the woman's extravagant gesture is in fact a prompt for us to act in their behalf.

* It's a tiny detail, but the Greek text doesn't actually read that the poor "you will always have with you" (future tense) but "you always have with you" (present tense). Jesus isn't making a future prediction, but rather stating a sad fact.

21

People sometimes asked Jesus to "work a sign" to prove his claims. Why didn't he do what they asked to make believing easier (see Matthew 12:38–42, Luke 11:29–32)?

You are right; whenever Jesus is asked to perform some mighty work as proof that he is who he says he is, his response is always no. If I had been put in the same spot, I would have pulled out every trick I had to score points with my audience.*

Jesus's unwillingness to prove himself is puzzling unless he was trying to do something beyond winning folks over by razzle dazzle. When it might be to God's advantage to yank us about like puppets, instead we are wooed and invited. God, then, is more like a parent of adult children than a puppeteer—working more by nudges and hints and less by brute force. And, evidently, so is God's Son.

When Jesus performed mighty works, it was to demonstrate that God's Reign is breaking in (see Matthew 12:28) and to lead people to a change of heart (see Matthew 11:20). After all, "to gather into one the dispersed children of God" (John 11:52)—not performing magic on request—was his purpose for coming.

---

* Jesus also never used his power for his own comfort. Think of his refusal to turn stones into bread when he was hungry (see Matthew 4:2–4) and his prayer "not what I will but what you will" (Mark 14:36) in the garden before his death.

22

Does the Bible really teach that women should be submissive to men (see Ephesians 5:21)?

Well, yes and no. From 1,000 BC through AD 100, the time period when the writings that became the Bible were composed and collected, men led in the society of the Mediterranean world. A husband and father's word was law; the duty of wife and children was to obey. A woman without father, husband, or adult son was something of a non-person. This explains why care for widows was God's measure of a just society (see Exodus 22:21, James 1:27). That the early Church grew up in this environment and reflected these values is seen in the instruction that appears a handful of times in the New Testament: "Wives should be subordinate to their husbands as to the Lord" (Ephesians 5:22; see Colossians 3:18, 1 Peter 3:1–2). But it's far from clear whether this arrangement is God's eternal plan for the genders and family or an accident of time and culture. For there is another side to the story.

We have mentioned before that Jesus was something of a line-crosser when it came to matters of Jewish ritual rules,* and to some degree that was the case in his treatment of women. Though it was normal in first-century Judaism to educate only men in the fine points of the Law, Jesus numbered women among his disciples (see Luke 8:1–3). He developed an unusual teacher-student relationship with Mary and Martha, Lazarus's sisters (see Luke 10:38–42, John 11:19–27), and the Samaritan woman at the well (see John, chapter 4). Saint Paul also named women coworkers (see Romans 16:3), apostles (see Romans 16:7), and those who "have struggled at my side in promoting the gospel" (Philippians 4:3).

And often overlooked, Paul's words that "wives should be subordinate to their husbands" come only after an earlier command addressed to men and women alike: "Be subordinate to one another out of reverence for Christ" (Ephesians 5:21). Being subordinate, then, is Paul's general plea for his readers to be like Jesus himself—humble, attentive, and willing to take the last place.

So far it would seem that the Bible offers ammunition for both sides of the question. But, for me, the definitive argument in listening to Paul on the relations between wives and husbands comes in a line about another uneven relationship in his day: "Slaves, be obedient to your human masters" (Ephesians 6:5). It took us eighteen centuries to get it, but Christians came to see that Paul's acceptance of his culture's attitude toward slaves was inconsistent with the principles of the Gospel. Is it not also likely that the Bible's view on the relationship between men and women should be treated in the same way—as a reflection of a particular historical time, and not as God's everlasting command?

* See question 8 in this section.

23

Is the Book of Revelation really about the end of the world (see Revelation, chapters 6, 8–9, 16)?

The final book of the Bible offers us a vision of the ultimate defeat of Satan and the final victory of God's will over all, but Catholics do not read it as a timetable or countdown for the end of time. Nor, frankly, do most other Christians, though the variety of television preachers and end-of-the-world books available might make you think otherwise.*

Again the place to start in reading a biblical book is to ask, "What kind of writing is this? What did the inspired author intend?"** Though Revelation may seem to be one of a kind, there is actually a whole body of similar writings by Jews and Christians composed around the same time (the first century AD) that can help us understand it. Like the Book of Revelation, these other works feature a heavenly messenger coming to announce to hassled believers that God has seen their trials and will soon bring relief to them and judge their enemies. In the meantime, the readers are encouraged to hang tough and be faithful.

Scholars have given this kind of writing a name: apocalyptic literature. By noting all these resemblances, you get to see that those who use apocalyptic literature to foretell the future are missing the author's point (as has happened repeatedly with Revelation in the second, thirteenth, nineteenth, and twentieth centuries). Though Revelation does speak of God's ultimate plan, John the Seer is speaking not just to people of some future day, but to believers of every day and age, for Christ's followers will always face spiritual and sometimes physical enemies.

Do you remember the opening scene of the original *Star Wars* movie? Darth Vader and his storm troopers have boarded the ship of Princess Leia, who has been carrying plans for the Empire's new Death Star to the Resistance. Darth is machine-like, ominously clothed in black, and his cohorts seem less like humans than robots. On the other hand, Princess Leia, dressed all in white, is a real looker. Her crew (and for all their goofiness, even her droids) seem more, well, human. In the first few minutes of the movie, we already know whom to root for. Regardless of the seeming invincibility of the Empire, in the end Mr. D. Vader will not prevail. We are being urged to align ourselves with the Force.

With its fantastic imagery and intermeshed visions, the Book of Revelation is less a countdown to the end of time than it is the Bible's version of *Star Wars*. It speaks to every generation of Christians to remain firm in the face of every opposition. Regardless of the power of the horsemen, the plagues, the Red Dragon, the Beast from the Sea, and the other forces ranged against God's faithful few, there's no doubt how the contest will end. God controls the reins of history and will bring about the ultimate victory of life over death.

* For more about the Rapture, the anti-Christ, and the like, see questions 10 and 11 in section 3.

** See question 9 in section 1.

Section 3: FAQs on Challenges About the Catholic Faith

Have you noticed that when some people find out you are Roman Catholic, they are suddenly full of questions? Mention that you have an obligation to the youth group at Saint Who-zit's Church or that you are a student at Saint What-zit's School, and all of a sudden you find yourself being quizzed. I can think of several reasons why.

Sometimes when people have questions about your faith, it really means they want to learn more about you. When we meet an intriguing personality for the first time, we pepper the person with questions about tastes in music, sports interests, family, and the like. It's all part of getting to know him or her. Asking someone about his or her religious practice can be part of that. If people do this to you, I hope you see it as good news.

Sometimes when people have questions about your religious practice, it's a sign they are hungry for God themselves. In some homes, Mom and Dad have accidentally, or intentionally, avoided the subject. Rather than just blurting out, "I have all sorts of questions about God because I didn't learn anything at home," people often ask their peers what they believe (especially if the peers seem rather at home with it). So it could be that someone's needs and your gifts have intersected. This is what we in the God business term a *calling.* Don't panic; just try to express what God and faith mean to you, and see where it leads.

But sometimes when people have questions about your Catholic faith, it may be that they aim to talk you out of it and into something else. Because we are such a large Church with roots going back to Christ and the Apostles, Catholicism is to some people the Microsoft or McDonald's of religions. The Catholic way is the backdrop against which they define themselves. So they have lots of often very pointed questions: "Why do you Catholics worship Mary . . . have statues in your churches . . . refuse to read the Bible . . . think you can buy your way to heaven?" and on and on. You get the sense they believe they already know quite a bit about our faith, are disturbed by certain aspects of it, and are concerned for the salvation of your soul. This can be very uncomfortable. But this too is a *calling*—a meeting of another's needs with your abilities—and it can be a good thing.

A little research on your part may be called for. The point of this final section is to help you understand your own faith and give you some words to explain it better to those who are asking about it. I hope you will care enough to share what you believe. Christ is counting on it, and Saint Peter was thinking of you when he wrote, "Always be ready to give an explanation to anyone who asks you for a reason for your hope" (1 Peter 3:15b).

By now I would suspect you are aware of my way of operating. Each question and response is as independent of the others as possible, though at times I recommend that you look back to check out other questions and answers that offer some background on the matter at hand.

1

My friend says the Bible should be our only guide to God, quoting 2 Timothy 3:14–17, and wants to know why so many Catholic beliefs and practices have so little to do with the Bible. What do I say?

Your friend is assuming that the Bible, God's written Word, is God's only and last Word. Catholics just don't see it that way.

Back in the sixteenth century, some people were calling for serious reform in the Church. They felt that the Pope and bishops were failing to be true to Christ. So in the place of the living direction of the Church's hierarchy, they promoted the text of the Bible as the only trustworthy guide. "The Bible alone" ("*sola scriptura*" in Latin) became their rally cry. This explains something you may have noticed about some of your non-Catholic friends who are into their faith—they don't do *anything* without the Bible. They carry it with them just about everywhere, have memorized Scripture verses to guide them, and use God's Word as the touchstone for making decisions.

As far as that goes, it's a great thing and a habit (frankly) I wish more Catholics would adopt, but something is missing. The idea that everything we need to know about God and faith is in the Bible isn't actually *in* the Bible. It's an idea some impose on it. Lots of verses hail that God's written Word is powerful and life-giving, like the one your friend offered: "All scripture is inspired by God and is useful for teaching, for refutation, for correction, and for training in righteousness" (2 Timothy 3:16). But none of them, including this verse from 2 Timothy, claim that the Bible is the only and complete source of faith for Christians or the only way God has chosen to show himself.

As we've seen, the Bible is complex and there are always new questions to bring to it, but what good is a library, even an inspired one, if no one is sure how to interpret it? If you want some evidence that the Bible, all by itself, cannot lead us to the fullness of truth, check out "Churches" in the yellow pages of a big city phone directory. You'll find a variety of Christian groups listed—including a bunch who take the Scriptures alone as their guide. Even these groups find in God's library different, and often contradictory, answers to life's problems. If the Bible is supposed to work as our *only* guide, shouldn't we hope for a little more agreement among its readers? Something more than a divinely inspired writing by itself seems necessary.

And God provides. At his Last Supper, Jesus promised to send us another living helper: "I have much more to tell you, but you cannot bear it now. But when he comes, the Spirit of truth, he will guide you to all truth" (John 16:12–13a).* So when Jesus returned to the Father, he didn't leave a reading list, but rather a Spirit-filled community, led by the Apostles. Their preaching and reflecting on Jesus form the Catholic Church's living Tradition, some of which was eventually written down to become the New Testament. And it's the bishops and the Pope, the successors to Peter and the Apostles, who continue to interpret the Scriptures and Tradition for our time under the guidance of the Holy Spirit. Catholics recognize the need for not only an inspired book but also an inspired interpreter.

* See also John 14:17,26; 15:26.

2

So Roman Catholics don't really base their faith on the Bible?

Oh, no, no, no. Catholics *are* a biblical Church; we just aren't a Bible-*only* Church. This is at the root of why some Christians have issues with our faith. Let me repeat myself a little: though most Catholic beliefs and practices are rooted in the Bible, and none of them could conflict with it, we think this inspired book requires an inspired interpreter. The Scriptures are not "Jesus's Little Instruction Manual" for building a church, but are the earliest Christians' graced reflections on God's saving work for them.* For every subsequent generation of believers, then, the Bible remains as God's gift to us, providing a compass, a guide, and a doorway to the divine.

Remember me talking earlier about the Bible as a bicycle shop?** Just as I can find everything I need to outfit me to ride there *except* the knowledge of how actually to do it, so the Bible makes available all I need for a disciple's life *except* the knack of how to interpret it. That fuller understanding of what God is up to is what Catholics mean by Tradition (note the capital "T" here). The point that not all of God's saving truth was handed on in written form is often made in the New Testament: "Therefore, brothers, stand firm and hold fast to the traditions that you were taught, either by an oral statement or by a letter of ours" (2 Thessalonians 2:15).***

Catholics often rely on the living transmission of God's truth that is Tradition to express in a few carefully chosen words what the Bible says at greater length. For example, the statement that Jesus is "totally human and totally divine" captures what the whole of Scripture is trying to say about Jesus, though the exact words aren't found there. It's an element of Catholic Tradition.

In the same way, the Spirit-driven process by which the Church came to accept these seventy-three books and only these seventy-three as God-inspired words is an example of Tradition as well.

So Catholics don't blush over accepting certain things as God's truth even though they are not explicitly found in the Scriptures. We know them as part of the fuller picture that Jesus had in mind when, at the Last Supper, he promised his disciples an Advocate who would teach us everything (see John 14:26). Our God continues to lead us to understand better and better what he has done and is doing for us. For Catholics, then, it's not "the Bible alone" but the Scriptures *and* Tradition through which God speaks to his people.

* Perhaps it has never dawned on you, but the first generations of Christians didn't have a written New Testament. They began the process that helped compose it.

** See question 11 in section 1.

*** See other positive words from Paul about oral tradition in 1 Corinthians 11:2 and 2 Timothy 2:2.

3

My friend says that in Mark 7:8, Jesus warns that human traditions get in the way of God's Word and that Catholics believe in Tradition. How do I respond?

Your friend is partially right. Jesus did get tired of religious folks whose little rules ended up smothering God's clearly stated intentions. In the story in chapter 7 of Mark, Jesus is hassled by some Jewish leaders over his disciples' failure to prayerfully wash their hands before eating. It is in this context that Jesus says, "You disregard God's commandment but cling to human tradition" (verse 8). Jesus's problem with "human traditions" isn't with the *tradition* part but with the *human* part. Like the prophets before him, Jesus has no patience for those who use manmade rules to dodge divine obligations. But he also instructs his disciples to abide by traditions that don't conflict with God's rules.*

We must always guard against confusing God's desires with our own ways of doing things. Lots of the habits and customs Christians use to express their faith (what we could call *tradition* with a small "t") can and will differ. For example, the practice of making the Sign of the Cross by touching your left shoulder and then your right (the Eastern Church makes the gesture right over left) and which days Catholics celebrate as holy days of obligation are small "t" traditions that give practical shape to our faith. But God did not decide these things and, if thought necessary, the Church could change them. On the other hand, aspects of our faith like the Nicene Creed, the official list of books in the Bible, and our understanding of Christ's real presence in the Eucharist are examples of Sacred Tradition (with a capital "T") that have their origins with the Apostles and are eternally true.

* See Matthew 23:1–3 for an example.

4

According to the Bible, "A person is justified by faith apart from works of the law" (Romans 3:28). I have a friend who keeps asking, "Why do Catholics believe they need to 'earn' heaven by doing good works?" How do I explain this?

This is a place where we need to watch our mouths. I mean, the reason that Protestant friends may accuse Catholics of thinking we can buy our way to heaven is that at times some of us seem to talk that way. When questioned about our prospects for eternal life, our knee-jerk response may be: "Well, I *hope* to get to heaven. I mean, I've tried to be a good person." See? At first blush it may sound like we assume our chances at salvation are based on a business deal: *Do something for God, and God will do something for you.* This probably isn't what you mean, and it certainly isn't what the Catholic Church teaches.

But this is how the world sometimes works. You know, happy babies get held more than crabby ones. The folks seem more pleased to see us when we bring home a good report card or score the winning goal than when we announce we are on academic probation or explain how we struck out with bases loaded in the bottom of the ninth (again). We get the picture— perform and people will like you.

The big mistake we sometimes make is thinking that God operates the same way. The cultural philosophy of "I'll love you as long as you do what I want you to do" is challenged by the Christian vision: "God proves his love for us in that while we were still sinners Christ died for us" (Romans 5:8). Grace is what we call it: finding out that we are loved not because of our performance, but despite it. So with all other Christians, then,

Catholics put their final confidence in God's promises and the saving work of Jesus. We cannot buy our way into God's affections. Nor need we. As a famous preacher named Paul Tillich put it, "Accept the fact that you are accepted" (*The Shaking of the Foundations*, page 162). Faith opens the door.

But Jesus reminded us that something more than nice words is called for to get us through the door: "Not everyone who says to me, 'Lord, Lord,' will enter the kingdom of heaven, but only the one who does the will of my Father in heaven" (Matthew 7:21). So thinking about God correctly and trusting in Christ must lead to cooperating with God in acts of love. Or again, in some well-chosen words from James:

> What good is it, my brothers, if someone says he has faith but does not have works? Can that faith save him? If a brother or sister has nothing to wear and has no food for the day, and one of you says to them, "Go in peace, keep warm, and eat well," but you do not give them the necessities of the body, what good is it? So also faith of itself, if it does not have works, is dead. (James 2:14–17)

So trying to be a good person *does* have a place—but as a response to our already being loved by God, not as any attempt to earn it. So, true to the Bible, Catholics think it's not either/or but both trusting God *and* acting uprightly that matter. As Saint Paul put it, all that counts for anything is "faith working through love" (Galatians 5:6).

5

My friend asks: "The Bible tells us that if we believe in Jesus, we can be sure we are going to heaven (see 1 John 5:13). So why aren't you Catholics more sure that you're going to heaven?"

I wouldn't say we are *sure,* but we are *hopeful.* Wanting to see God face to face is how the Bible talks about life's goal (see 1 Corinthians 13:12), and Catholics share that hope with every other Christian, but we are a little taken aback by the casualness with which some seem to speak about having a reservation in heaven all sewn up. Because Catholics and Protestants have different ways of understanding how one comes to know God's saving work,* we have different ways of talking about our hope for heaven.

As Catholics read it, the New Testament speaks about "being saved" as a drama in three acts: one part something already accomplished, one part something happening now, and one part something yet to be. "For by grace you have been saved" (Ephesians 2:8) and God "has saved us and called us to a holy life" (2 Timothy 1:9) are a couple representative passages that speak about the saving work Christ has already accomplished for us on the cross. But in other places, Paul talks about our eternal destiny as something not yet settled. For example, he refers to believers as those "being saved" (1 Corinthians 1:18) and likens his own standing with God to an athletic contest: "I drive my body and train it, for fear that, after having preached to others, I myself should be disqualified" (1 Corinthians 9:27). It's something he continues to strive for, lest he lose it. Finally, he talks about salvation as something we will possess for good only in the future: "How much more then, since we are now justified by his blood, will we be saved through him" (Romans 5:9).

So God's saving work in us extends over the past, present, and future. Those Christians who seem so very sure of their spot in heaven put most of their weight on the "past thing" salvation references, downplaying the present and future aspects. "God's saving work has been accomplished," they say, "so we can be assured of heaven."

Catholics give equal weight to all three tenses. Yes, Christ's dying and rising, the ultimate expression of God's love for us and ransom for our sin, opened heaven's gates. For this finished work, Catholics use the word *redemption*. But true disciples are called to cooperate with that grace right now through a life of devotion and right living. And the remnants of sin continue to have a nasty grip on our hearts after Baptism, so Catholics think it a little brash to count ourselves "saved" until we've lived our lives of discipleship through and had God declare it so on Judgment Day. So the quick Catholic (and biblical) response to those who ask, "Are you saved?" is "No, but I am redeemed; and like Saint Paul, I'm working out my salvation" (see Philippians 2:12).

* See question 4 in this section.

One of my friends asked me, "Are you 'born again' (see John 3:1–7)?" I told her, "Yes, I was born anew when I was baptized as a baby." She didn't seem impressed. Did I say something wrong?

Actually, you answered well. Thanks to the Bible, almost all Christians have the same story of how things stand between God and us: God created humans out of love and for love, but something in us is deep in rebellion against God. We also agree on the remedy: Christ's dying and rising has bridged the gap, and by faith we receive the healing medicine of this saving action. But Christians have varying ways of understanding what comes next. You see this in how differently we interpret these words of Jesus to Nicodemus: "No one can see the kingdom of God without being born from above" (John 3:3).*

What your friend likely meant by "Are you born again?" is "Have you made a mature decision for Christ?" This is what they believe Jesus expects—a decisive moment when, after a period of going on our own way, we face our isolation and let God in. They may describe it as "choosing Christ" or "accepting Jesus as my Lord and Savior." It's often a dramatic, emotional moment they can pinpoint on a calendar. Think of a light switch turning on. And it's important because, as they understand it, this is what makes you a Christian. Without a born-again experience to report, you don't yet know (they say) God's saving grace.

But that just isn't our story. Catholics believe we participate in God's life, become a Christian, and are "born from above," when we're baptized. We get that idea from Jesus, for a few verses later in John's Gospel, as a synonym for "being born from above," he says, "No one can enter the kingdom of God without being born of water and Spirit" (3:6). Salvation, as Catholics understand it, unfolds over time in our response to God's grace-filled steps toward us. That's one of the best things about the Church's practice of baptizing the newborn infants of believing parents; it downplays our efforts (a baby, you will have to agree, can't do much of anything "productive") and emphasizes that we receive God's life as a gift. For Catholics the key isn't a *moment* when we decide for Jesus, but a *process* of gradually waking up, responding to Christ in ways that bring us closer and finally allow us to imitate Jesus. Coming to salvation is less like a light switch being turned on and more like a seed sprouting: putting down a root, raising a green finger, having growth spurts and dormant periods, and in time bearing fruit.

There are people who, after living without making much room for God, have a definitive faith turnaround. (Some of them are even Catholics!) But with Christ a decision is not the end, but just the beginning. Though we as Catholics hold ourselves as "born anew" from Baptism, the work of growing in holiness (what is called sanctification) will take us our whole lives.

* The Greek word for "from above" can also be translated as "again."

7

My friend asks, "Why don't Catholics ever talk about having a relationship with Jesus?" Well, do we?

Catholics *do* talk about having a relationship with Jesus, but perhaps not as clearly as we should. Jesus, the Son of God, broke new ground when he addressed his disciples, "I have called you friends" (John 15:15). This was a bold concept at the time; when the Old Testament talks about our relationship with God, parent and child, ruler and subject images dominate. It's from Jesus's lead that Christians started describing their connection to God as a friendship. The fourth-century writer Saint Gregory Nazianzen described his life's goal "to be, rather than to seem to be, a friend of God." And the *Catechism of the Catholic Church* repeatedly describes our life with God as a friendship.* It's fair to say Christ wants nothing more, but nothing less, than that.

Stop and think about what friends do for friends. They spend time together by intention, not chance. They don't let other things—even attractive things—get in the way. They learn more about each other. They bare their hearts to each other and influence each other. They stand by each other, even when it's inconvenient. Time, knowledge, openness, loyalty—not a bad description of a disciple, is it? And in receiving Christ's own Body and Blood in the Eucharist, taking him into ourselves, our Friend becomes part of us. So being Catholic does indeed mean having a relationship with Jesus.

*See numbers 277, 374, 396, and 1468.

8

My friend asks, "The Bible says we should worship God alone (see Revelation 19:10), so why do Catholics pray to Mary?"

This is one of those places where Catholics may sometimes give others the wrong impression. We don't really pray *to* Mary as much as we pray *with* her, and she with us. So the place to start is by noticing a couple things about praying for one another that we may take for granted.

First, we are commanded to do it. Jesus orders us to ask and seek and knock, and promises to give whatever we ask in his name (see Luke 11:9 and John 14:13–14). When you consider that God knows our needs better than we ourselves do, that encouragement to bring our needs before God is itself pretty amazing. C. S. Lewis suggested that in giving us this charge, Jesus would honor his disciples by allowing them to share in his own creative and saving work.

Second, after accepting the call to pray for our needs, inviting others to join us is a natural thing. Saint Paul tells his readers he is praying for them (see Romans 1:9–10 and Philippians 1:4 for starters) and isn't bashful about asking them to pray for him (see Colossians 4:3 and 1 Thessalonians 5:25). And if friends and family can join us in prayer, how much more helpful would it be to invite those who are already with God to join us? The Book of Revelation mentions angels presenting "the prayers of the saints" before the heavenly throne (5:8 NRSV; see 8:3–5). Our Christian ancestors have always welcomed the powerful praying help of the angels and saints.

In her openness to do God's will, we count Mary as the first disciple and the first of all God's saints. It's little wonder then that the Mother of Jesus is a favorite prayer partner for Catholics. To be precise though, we pray *to* Mary in the sense that we are asking her to pray *with* us and *for* us.

So let's bring all this to a prayer that most Catholics learn, the *Ave Maria,* or Hail Mary. The first two lines are from the New Testament. When the angel Gabriel announces to Mary God's plan for bringing the Savior to birth, he greets her: "Hail, favored one! The Lord is with you" (Luke 1:28). The prayer just adds her name, Mary, to this greeting. In the very next scene, Mary's relative Elizabeth greets the new mother of the Messiah with what will become the prayer's second line: "Blessed are you among women, and blessed is the fruit of your womb" (Luke 1:42). The last part of the Hail Mary adds our request that Mary join us in bringing our needs to God: "Holy Mary, Mother of God, pray for us sinners, now and at the hour of our death." That's it: two lines from the Gospel, and a request to join us in prayer.

Our Protestant friends fear that Catholics sometimes mix up Mary's part in this with God's role. There's nothing mixed up about it. As we would naturally invite others to keep our needs in prayer, we ask Mary, the first of the disciples, to join us in bringing our needs before God.

9

My friend asks: "Why do your churches have statues? The Bible says, 'You shall not carve idols for yourselves in the shape of anything'" (Exodus 20:4).

Your friend has noticed something that you may have taken for granted. Catholics know that beauty is one of God's best things, so we accessorize our prayer places with stained glass, statuary, and art. Most Protestant churches in America, though often beautiful in their own way, are usually much plainer in décor and do not include statues and images. Unlike Catholic churches, even the cross that may be the centerpiece of a Protestant sanctuary is usually bare.

Some of the sixteenth-century Protestant reformers feared that art in church distracted people from God and violated the Ten Commandments. In addition to forbidding the worship of other gods, the Israelites were indeed ordered to "not carve idols for yourselves in the shape of anything" (Exodus 20:4) and to "not bow down before them or worship them" (Exodus 20:5). That seems pretty clear, except that in the rest of the Old Testament, God goes on to command Moses to make images of angel figures, called cherubim (see Exodus 25:18–20), and a serpent (see Numbers 21:8–9), and commands King David to fashion a lid for the ark of the Covenant with more cherubim (see 1 Chronicles 28:18–19).

As Catholics read it, the real concern of the First Commandment is not the making of such items in themselves, but *worshiping* them—giving them the honor God alone is owed. The word for that, in times ancient and modern, is *idolatry*. We use religious art to remind us of God's presence in the same way photos of relatives remind us of the ones we love. In the eyes of

Catholics, it looks like some Christians got a little carried away in stripping their churches of art and whitewashing the walls.

Catholics properly use beautiful representations of Jesus himself as well as biblical and Christian heroes as reminders and encouragements. Having said that, there can be a risk of confusing the pointer (the artwork) with the real thing (the object of your love). We should always look beyond the gift to the Giver.

10 My friend asks, "Where did you Catholics come up with Purgatory?"

Well, it's in the Bible. Not the actual word, mind you, but the idea. As I've mentioned before,* sometimes our ancestors coined words to say quickly what the Bible takes a long time to say. For example, the idea of God's being three Persons in one: Trinity. That word isn't in the Bible, but it's what the Bible says. So with Purgatory.

Direct your friend to the twelfth chapter of the Second Book of Maccabees. Now there may be a problem: your friend's Bible may not include 2 Maccabees. Catholics use the forty-six-book Old Testament inherited from the first Christians; most Protestants use a shorter thirty-nine-book list with links to Jewish practice that does not include 2 Maccabees. Sometimes this makes a difference. An idea that might not be found in a Protestant version of God's library may well exist in our larger Catholic one.

Anyway, 2 Maccabees mentions a sacrifice for forgiveness that a Jewish general offers at the temple for his fallen soldiers. The narrator comments:

> In doing this he acted in a very excellent and noble way, inasmuch as he had the resurrection of the dead in view; for if he were not expecting the fallen to rise again, it would have been useless and foolish to pray for them in death. . . . Thus he made atonement for the dead that they might be freed from this sin. (12:43b–44,46)

Throughout most of the Old Testament, God's people had no hope of a life after death. But when 2 Maccabees was written—a century and a half before Jesus—some Jews not only hoped for a resurrection but also believed God could make righteous those who were less than perfect when they died. That's the heart of what the Catholic Church means by Purgatory.

Here's another way to think about it. Because God is perfect, there's no room with God for wimpiness and sin. The Book of Revelation says as much when it says that nothing unclean will enter heaven (see 21:27). If my life ended today, yes, I would die as God's beloved son, but I would also still be more than a little self-interested, weak, and sinful. I'd be forgiven, but not full grown. For me to enjoy the fullness that God has in store will likely call for a lot of stretching and purifying. That act of love by which God continues to purify those who have trusted in him and have lived according to his paths is what Catholics mean by Purgatory.** It's not a place (like Toledo), but a process (like growing up). It means we're being readied to see God face to face. It's a very good thing.

* See questions 2 and 3 in this section.

** Note the word *continues*. Purgatory is really our hope that the growing up process into holy perfection that we are engaged in right now can be finished even after our death.

11

My friend asks, "Why don't Catholics talk about the Rapture the Bible speaks about in 1 Thessalonians 4:16–17?"

Catholics don't talk about the Rapture the way some Christians do because, frankly, it's a very new idea that doesn't reach back to Jesus or the Apostles. Though Tradition helps Catholics express God's truth in a fuller way in new situations, it doesn't give the Church authority to add new teaching without historic roots.

Some Bible readers spend lots and lots of energy trying to decipher hidden meanings they think lie beneath the Bible's words and visions about the end of time. A nineteenth-century English clergyman, John Darby, combined some speculations about a vision in the Book of Revelation of Christ's thousand-year reign (see 20:1–8) with his own view of a passage from Paul's First Letter to the Thessalonians (see 4:16–17). Darby proposed that God would *rapture*—that is, "take away"—all true believers before the terrible disasters he thought the Bible predicted would happen before the final coming of Jesus Christ. Even though no Christian had heard of that idea in the previous eighteen centuries, the Rapture has caught on in a major way among some Protestants and even the popular culture.

Though Catholics do believe that Christ one day will establish his Reign over us and that those who have died before his final coming will not miss out—what Paul was trying to tell the Thessalonians—we don't talk of the Rapture. Nor, for that matter, do we spend lots of energy trying to predict what Jesus himself admitted not knowing (see Mark 13:32): when the end of the world will come.

12 | If we believe God is good and loving, how can we believe in hell?

This is one of those moments where the Bible seems at first to clash with itself. On the one hand, Jesus speaks of the Father's, and his own, love and saving desire for us (see Luke 19:10, John 3:16–17); on the other hand, he doesn't shy away from warning of the judgment awaiting those who want nothing to do with God's saving work (see Mark 9:42–48, Matthew 23:29–38). I said the Bible *seems* to clash with itself in speaking of a loving God who also supports the enterprise we call hell,* but a little clear thinking about love may help here.

Love always wants what is best for the other, but if the other is mature and sane, a necessary element of love is freedom. I might think I would be a great friend to you, but if you don't want my friendship, my pushing myself onto you is just another kind of violence. Just so, God respects our freedom so much that he would never force himself onto us. C. S. Lewis, who often has a wonderful way of explaining hard things, suggests that in the end, it comes down to one of two options: (1) either we say to God "your will be done" (Do you hear the echo of the Lord's Prayer there?), or (2) out of respect for our free choices, God will regretfully have to say to us, "Your will be done." In the truest sense, God sends no one to hell; we choose it ourselves by not wanting God in our lives.

One more thing. Though the Church teaches that we have it in our power to deliberately turn away from God's invitation to friendship forever, we don't know that anyone who has walked this earth has ever done so. We all might have our favorite candidates for hell but, thankfully, the responsibility for judgment is not ours. We never know what God's grace might have been able to effect in a person's final moments.

Pope John Paul II wondered about this very thing:

> Can God, who has loved man so much, permit the man who rejects him to be condemned to eternal torment? . . . The silence of the church is, therefore, the only appropriate position for Christian faith. Even when Jesus says of Judas, the traitor, 'It would be better for that man if he had never been born' (Mt. 26:24), his words do not allude for certain to eternal damnation. (*Crossing the Threshold of Hope*, pages 185–186)

It is surely a fine thing, then, to pray that hell is empty of human souls.

---

* In the Gospels, the actual word Jesus uses for the destination of sinners is *gehenna* (see Matthew 5:22,29; 23:15,33; Mark 9:43–45; Luke 12:5), which is sometimes translated as "hell." *Gehenna* was literally the Valley of Hinnom, a ravine just outside the city that served as Jerusalem's dumping ground. Complete with rotting garbage, smoldering fires, and little animals that live on dying things, it's a very vivid picture of a bad end. No sinner will literally go to the Valley of Hinnom (now a suburb of Jerusalem), but you get the picture.

My friend says the Bible claims that only people who believe in Jesus go to heaven. What do you think?

We need to be careful here, for the Bible speaks about this with different voices that *together,* like harmony in music, express the whole truth. Our Church would hold onto everything the Bible says on the matter.

The Scriptures state in several ways that Jesus is the one means of access to divine life. Jesus himself says it clearly at the Last Supper: "I am the way and the truth and the life. No one comes to the Father except through me" (John 14:6).* But there are other verses in the Bible that speak of God's desire to save all, even those who don't know the Son. For example, Saint Paul marvels that God's truth is found even in those who haven't been instructed: "For when the Gentiles who do not have the law by nature observe the prescriptions of the law, they are a law for themselves. . . . They show that the demands of the law are written in their hearts" (Romans 2:14–15a).**

Some folks are impressed with the first truth, insisting that only those who actively and knowingly profess Christ will be saved. Others put their theological eggs in the second view, trusting that all roads somehow lead to God.

The bishops at the Second Vatican Council thought hard about the matter and gave Catholics a balanced response to the question. Affirming that Jesus is our best window on God, through whom salvation comes, they wrote:

> Christ, present to us in His Body, which is the Church, is the one Mediator and the unique way of salvation. In explicit terms He Himself affirmed the necessity of faith and baptism (cf. Mark 16:16; John 3:5) and thereby affirmed

also the necessity of the Church, for through baptism as through a door men enter the Church. (*Dogmatic Constitution on the Church,* number 14)

But recognizing that God's grace acts in mysterious ways, beyond the confines of those who explicitly profess faith in Jesus, they added a little later: "Those also can attain to salvation who through no fault of their own do not know the Gospel of Christ or His Church, yet sincerely seek God and moved by grace strive by their deeds to do His will as it is known to them through the dictates of conscience" (number 16).

When they went on to speak of the Jewish people, Muslims, and other religious people, the bishops chose to speak of what they share with Christians, while also calling on believers to bring the fullness of the Good News in Jesus to them.

So Christ is the sure way, and we have no other. That's why we work hard to spread knowledge of Jesus. But God's grace is everywhere, and it's possible that even those who do not know Jesus himself may cooperate with it and perhaps be saved.

* For verses that point to Jesus as our one and only means to salvation, see also Mark 16:15–16, Acts of the Apostles 4:12, and 1 Timothy 2:5–6a.

** For verses that hint at God's salvific will, even for those who do not know Jesus explicitly, see also Acts of the Apostles 10:34–35, 1 Timothy 2:3–4, and 1 John 4:16.

14. My friend asks, "Why does the Church discourage Catholics from reading the Bible?"

Well, if you have worked your way through fifty questions about how Catholics think biblically, I hope you see that something is just wrong about this question. Listen to these words from the *Catechism of the Catholic Church:* "The Church 'forcefully and specifically exhorts all the Christian faithful . . . to learn the "surpassing knowledge of Jesus Christ," by frequent reading of the divine Scriptures'"[3] (number 133). But we are also urged to read the Bible *with* the Church.

Before the invention of printing in the fifteenth century and the subsequent growth in literacy, Bibles were rare and costly. Most Christians relied on teaching, preaching, and art to receive God's saving truth. With the divisions among Christians that came with the Reformation, many bishops and pastors hesitated to encourage their people to read the Scriptures on their own lest more confusion result. They took Saint Peter to heart when he wrote, "No prophecy of scripture is a matter of one's own interpretation" (2 Peter 1:20, NRSV), and encouraged Catholics to learn God's Word through catechisms and devotional books written by approved, knowledgeable teachers. Over time direct reading of the Bible became more associated with Protestants.

Happily, those times and most of their fears are behind us. Books are inexpensive, literacy is commonplace in most developed countries, and there are many helpful Bible study guides for Catholics. It looks to me like all our excuses are gone.

15

My friend asks, "Why do Catholics baptize babies instead of waiting until people can choose for themselves?"

It's clear that the first followers of Jesus were all adults. But the Apostle Paul baptized "households" (see Acts 15:15,33; 1 Corinthians 1:16), so we can surmise that children were very soon being baptized with their adult parents. Clearly there was no biblical rule *against* the Baptism of infants, but maybe the better place to begin is to consider what we hold Baptism does.

For some Christians, Baptism is less an act that makes a change so much as it confirms something that's already taken place. The really significant event for them may be being "born again"—a one-time powerful surrender to Jesus as Lord and Savior.* In churches of the Pentecostal persuasion, even more significant than Baptism by water is the personal reception of the Holy Spirit as demonstrated by speaking in tongues, a special prayer language. In these communities, being born again and personally receiving the Holy Spirit, not Baptism, makes you a Christian. It's only after undergoing one or the other that an individual may request Baptism as a way of ratifying her or his commitment to Christ.

The Catholic view of Baptism puts more emphasis on God's work at that moment than on our own. And things happen to us through Baptism: we are "born of water and Spirit" (John 3:5), we are "buried" with Christ and share "in newness of life" (Romans 6:3–4), and we are now "clothed . . . with Christ" (Galatians 3:27). The Eastern Orthodox and mainline Protestant churches that join us in baptizing infants and young children see it as a declaration that we do not earn our way into God's affections but receive God's love as gift. Before we can win a race, earn a buck, or do anything to be charming, God makes us adopted daughters and sons. God always takes the first step.**

But of course, an action that names us "God's own" before we are old enough to understand all that it means requires that someone keep affirming that truth in us as we grow. Short of that, Baptism would be like receiving a gift that we never unwrap. So the Catholic Church won't baptize a child if there aren't some important helpers who promise to introduce the new Christian in the coming years to the gift he or she has received. These will likely be parents, grandparents, and godparents, already strong in their own relationships with Christ. Sunday Mass, daily personal prayer, faith lessons from our parents, Confirmation preparation, and our parish's youth ministry all deepen our sense of what a tremendous thing God has done for us before we could do anything for ourselves.

* See question 6 in this section.

** For more on how Catholics balance God's free offer of a relationship with our need to cooperate with it, see question 7 in this section.

16

My friend says there is nothing in the Bible about confessing your sins to a priest. So why do Catholics think God's forgiveness comes only through confessing to a priest?

Obviously Jesus's whole mission was to heal the breach between God and us. So Catholics fill their days with all kinds of words and actions that seek and express God's forgiveness: we pray the Lord's Prayer ("forgive us our trespasses, as we forgive . . ."), examine our conscience, make Acts of Contrition, perform charitable works,* and fill every celebration of Mass with calls for forgiveness.** So God's forgiving grace is accessible to us in many ways, but we also have the Sacrament of Penance and Reconciliation.

There's a deep truth in the Bible that frightens some Christians. Though there might have been other ways, God has chosen to reach us by working *through* others. God used Moses to bring the Hebrew slaves to freedom. Jesus commissioned the Twelve and the seventy disciples to proclaim the Good News. And, in an astounding word, he identified himself with their efforts: "Whoever listens to you listens to me" (Luke 10:16a). No Christian I've ever met objects when another person acts as the proclaimer and channel of God's grace at Baptism. And Jesus specifically empowered his Apostles to continue his work of extending God's forgiveness when he breathed the Spirit on them on Easter night and said, "Whose sins you forgive are forgiven them" (John 20:23).

So why confess our sins to the Church's minister? *Because* sin is never a private thing, and expressing my failure to a representative of the whole Body of Christ makes it real. *Because*

I have a tendency to make mountains out of molehills (and mountains *into* molehills) and could use the advice of a wiser hand to help me gain perspective. *Because* I need help discerning how to lean on God more, and the priest will offer a suggestion (called a penance) to start me on that road. *Because,* though I may eloquently confess my sins in my bedroom each night, I often need to hear someone else say that God has indeed obliterated my sins. And, if all of these reasons don't do it for your friend, how about *because* the Bible says so: "Therefore, confess your sins to one another and pray for one another, that you may be healed" (James 5:16). Confession isn't the only road, but it is the superhighway of forgiveness.

* Think of Jesus's saying: "Give alms, and behold, everything will be clean for you" (Luke 11:41).

** Think, for starters, of the prayer of confession ("I confess to Almighty God . . ."), the "Lord, have mercy!" we use in the introductory rites, and the "Lord, I am not worthy to receive you, but only say the word and I shall be healed" prayer (based on Luke 7:6) we recite before receiving Communion.

17 My friend asks, "Why do you address your pastor as Father when in Matthew 23:9, Jesus says not to call anyone that?"

This is an example of a tendency of some to over-read the Bible. In a desire to respect one part of the text, we can fail to pay attention to the bigger biblical picture.

In a remark aimed at some religious leaders, Jesus said, "As for you, do not be called 'Rabbi.' You have but one teacher, and you are all brothers. Call no one on earth your father; you have but one Father in heaven" (Matthew 23:8–9). But if Jesus's point was truly to reserve the words *father* and *teacher* for God, someone failed to communicate the news to Saint Paul, who now and again refers to those who have the role of teachers in the churches (see Ephesians 4:11, 1 Corinthians 12:28) and refers to himself as the Corinthians' spiritual father (see 1 Corinthians 4:15). Even Matthew, in whose Gospel the warning about the title father appears, doesn't hesitate to use it when speaking of male parents (see, for example, 1:1–16, 4:21). Even Jesus uses it that way (10:21, 21:31)! It sounds to me that it's not the word itself that concerns him, but the baggage that may come with it.

In the whole passage, Jesus is fed up with the arrogance and insincerity that some leaders exhibit. Leadership, for Jesus, is all about service (see Matthew 23:11). The titles pastor and reverend are just as open to the same exaggeration as father or teacher. Religious leaders who are vain and conceited are the real issue for Jesus—not what words we use to address them.

18

My friend asks: "How can bread and wine become Jesus's Body and Blood? They still look and taste like bread and wine, don't they?"

Folks who claim to take the Bible fiercely word for word (for example, thinking Genesis, chapter 1, requires that you must believe in a seven-day Creation schedule) can sometimes switch gears and begin interpreting other verses figuratively without noticing what they've done. Your friend's question is an example. He or she likely comes from a religious tradition where Jesus's words at the Last Supper, "This is my body" (Mark 14:22), are understood poetically. But Catholics believe that bread and wine become the Lord's Body and Blood at the Eucharist because we take Jesus at his word.

A check on what Jesus meant at the Last Supper can be found in John's Gospel. He told those gathered in a synagogue, "I am the living bread that came down from heaven; whoever eats this bread will live forever; and the bread that I will give is my flesh for the life of the world" (6:51). The crowd grumbled, "How can this man give us [his] flesh to eat?" (6:52). They were stunned because they understood Jesus *literally*. But notice his response. He didn't say, "Oh, I didn't mean it that way" or "I was just kidding." No, he repeated himself for emphasis (see 6:53–58), leading many of his followers to cut and run.

The witness of the earliest Christian writings outside the New Testament confirms our interpretation that takes Jesus's Last Supper words at face value. For example, Ignatius of Antioch, in AD 110, wrote of certain people in his day who were confused about the matter: "They abstain from the eucharist . . . since they do not confess that the eucharist is the flesh of our savior Jesus Christ, which suffered on behalf of our sins and which the Father raised in his kindness" (Bart D. Ehrman, editor, *The Apostolic Fathers,* page 303). Similar comments from other writers like Justin, Origin, and Cyril of Jerusalem confirm that a figurative or poetic interpretation of Jesus's words does not reflect the practice of the earliest Church. Nor is it the outlook of contemporary Catholicism.

That the first Christians took the charge "Eat my body . . . drink my blood" seriously we can see. But just *how* the transformation happens is a mystery of God's doing. Thankfully Jesus commanded, "Take and eat," not, "Take and understand." But here's a Catholic way of thinking about it. Usually when things change, the core stuff remains unchanged even though the outer qualities are altered. Think of how you have grown from childhood—you are taller, heavier, better looking, but you remain you. Christ's presence in the Eucharist is unique in that although the taste, smell, and chemical makeup of the bread and wine remain the same, their heart (what theologians call their substance) becomes Christ's flesh and blood. So true to the Bible and the first generations of believers, Catholics hold that Christ is really present in the Eucharist (not just in our minds), but under the forms of bread and wine (not physically or chemically).

19

My friend points to the verse where it says, "We have been consecrated through the offering of the body of Jesus Christ once for all"(Hebrews 10:10), and then asks, "Why do Catholics think Jesus's sacrifice has to be repeated at every Mass?"

This question tends to leave most Catholics speechless. We certainly don't think we're making Jesus suffer over and over, so we're surprised when others tell us we are. The confusion comes with how the phrase "sacrifice of the Mass" strikes a Protestant ear.

Most ancient religions, including Old Testament Judaism, included as a major feature the gifting to God of animals, grain, incense, and, in some places, people, by killing or burning. One of the points the author to the Hebrews is making is that Jesus's gift of himself on the cross has made superfluous these repeated offerings. And Catholics agree. Jesus died only once (see Hebrews 7:27, 9:25–28, 10:10–14), entering "once for all into the sanctuary . . . with his own blood, thus obtaining eternal redemption" (Hebrews 9:12).

But what also needs to be said is that the power of this "eternal" gift is applied to us "in real time" when we obey Jesus's command to "Do this in memory of me" (Luke 22:19), the "this" being our representation through the Holy Spirit of Jesus's sacrificial death in a non-bloody, sacramental way. Catholics call the Mass a sacrifice because it is our connection to Christ's sacrifice of himself. The Crucifixion need never be repeated, but we can apply the power of that one sacrifice to ourselves every day through the Eucharist.

20

Where in the Bible do we find the Church's teachings on issues like abortion . . . the death penalty . . . why women aren't called to be priests . . . and . . . ?

These are some great questions, but we need to bring the Bible to them with care. Let's start by returning to something we mentioned at the outset.* The Bible is big because God is big. So God's library is also expansive, not easily defined or nailed down. Whenever anyone comes along with a verse from the Book of Nahum and claims, "Here is what the Bible says about [insert your favorite hot-button topic here]," you can be sure someone else will be able to come along with a verse from another spot in the Scriptures that seems to suggest something quite different.

Flipping through the Bible to find a verse to buttress our point of view (called prooftexting) is, unfortunately, a time-honored practice. What we often end up doing is imposing our own biases on God. How else did nineteenth-century preachers in the American south find a biblical justification for slavery in the story of Noah's cursing his grandson Ham (see Genesis 9:20–27)? How else do some contemporary readers of the Book of Revelation see the "mark of the beast" (as at Revelation 13:16–17) in the bar codes read by grocery store scanners? It's not likely that black slavery or the United Product Code were the real concerns of the authors of the books of Genesis and Revelation. Digging for a verse to back our point of view is no replacement for careful and prayerful reasoning about our faith. When it comes to the all-important "What would God want?" and "What would Jesus do?" questions, Catholics looks to the living authority of the Pope and bishops to lead us in that reflection, using every resource at hand, including, but not limited to, the Bible.

So on the matter of abortion, for example, Catholics start by asking what all people, by use of their reason, might come to affirm about the dignity of life, *and then* turn to the Scriptures for a corroborating and confirming word.** The Bible, then, often serves us better as a source for principles to build on than as a catalog of ready-to-use answers.

* See question 2 in section 1.

** See, for example, Jeremiah 1:5 and parts of Psalm 139.

21

Where should I go from here if I want to learn more about the Bible or how to explain my Catholic faith?

I am glad to hear that, even after all my words, you are still hungry for more. So many people seem to have gotten the impression that either you can be a religious person *or* an intelligent one. It seems to me you can't be one without the other. Keep wondering, for the more you understand something, the better you can love it.

Catholicism has been around for a long time and has been the religious home of some of the greatest minds in history. So if you have a question about an aspect of our faith, you can be sure (1) someone else has likely had the same concern before you, and (2) there are answers to be had. Here are a few resources that might help you in your quest to understand, listed in the order I think a high school student might find them helpful:

On FAQs About Using the Bible

God's Library: A Catholic Introduction to the World's Greatest Book, by Joe Paprocki (Loyola Press, 2002, 2005). An accessible overview of the biblical library, with reflection questions, tips for reading, and built-in "bookmark summaries" for your Bible.

The Seeker's Guide to Reading the Bible: A Catholic View, by Steve Mueller (Loyola Press, 1999). A more involved introduction, going over much of the same ground, still in the reach of the motivated high school student.

And God Said What? An Introduction to Biblical Literary Forms, by Margaret Nutting Ralph (Paulist Press, revised 2003). Just what the subtitle says, it will help you read the clues the biblical authors left so you can understand their message.

On FAQs on Tough Texts in the Bible

When someone brings together useful clues from language, history, and literary form to understand a text, you have a *commentary*. The footnotes you may find in your Bible are a sort of short commentary. A helpful way for Catholic readers to crack open challenging Bible passages is with the brief pamphlet commentaries on the individual books the Liturgical Press publishes as *The New Collegeville Bible Commentary*.

On FAQs on Challenges About the Catholic Faith

The Catholic Faith Handbook for Youth, by Brian Singer-Towns et al. (Saint Mary's Press, 2004). A guide to all the major teachings of the Catholic faith; in conformity with the *Catechism of the Catholic Church*.

Prove It! Church, by Amy Welborn (Our Sunday Visitor, 2001). Well-done, longer responses to sixteen typical questions written "with an attitude."

Born Fundamentalist, Born Again Catholic, by David Curie (Ignatius Press, 1996). An attractive way to learn how to explain your faith via the story of a young man's conversion from a conservative Christian outlook to Catholicism.

The New Question Box: Catholic Life in a New Century, by John J. Dietzen (Guildhall Publishers, 1997, 2002). Clear, sensitive, and amazingly brief answers to several hundred questions touching on all aspects of Catholic faith and practice.

Acknowledgments

The scriptural quotations marked NRSV are from the New Revised Standard Version of the Bible, Catholic Edition. Copyright © 1993 and 1989 by the Division of Christian Education of the National Council of the Churches of Christ in the United States of America. All rights reserved.

All other scriptural quotations in this book are from the New American Bible with Revised New Testament and Revised Psalms. Copyright © 1991, 1986, and 1970 by the Confraternity of Christian Doctrine, Washington, D.C. Used by the permission of the copyright owner. All rights reserved. No part of the New American Bible may be reproduced in any form without permission in writing from the copyright owner.

The quotations and excerpt on pages 24, 28, 45, and 101 are from the English translation of the *Catechism of the Catholic Church* for use in the United States of America, numbers 107, 110, 390, and 133, respectively. Copyright © 1994 by the United States Catholic Conference, Inc.—Libreria Editrice Vaticana. English translation of the *Catechism of the Catholic Church: Modifications from the Editio Typica* copyright © 1997, United States Catholic Conference, Inc.—Libreria Editrice Vaticana.

The quotation by Pope John Paul II on page 42 is from his address to the Pontifical Academy of Sciences, October 3, 1981, as reprinted in "John Paul II: Scripture and Science: The Path of Scientific Discovery," in *Origins*, volume 15, October 15, 1981, page 279.

The quotation by Paul Tillich on page 84 is from *The Shaking of the Foundations*, by Paul Tillich (New York: Charles Scribner's Sons), page 162. Copyright © 1948 by Charles Scribner's Sons.

The excerpt by Pope John Paul II on page 98 is from *Crossing the Threshold of Hope*, by John Paul II (New York: Alfred A. Knopf, 1994), pages 185–186. Copyright © 1994 by Arnoldo Mondadori Editore.

The excerpt and quotation on pages 99–100 and 100 are from *Dogmatic Constitution on the Church (Lumen Gentium),* numbers 14 and 16, at *www.vatican.va/archive/hist_councils/ii_vatican_council/documents/vat-ii_const_19641121_lumen-gentium_en.html,* accessed September 28, 2007.

The quotation by Ignatius on pages 107–108 is from *The Apostolic Fathers: I Clement, II Clement, Ignatius, Polycarp, Didache*, edited and translated by Bart D. Ehrman (Cambridge, MA: Harvard University Press, 2003), page 303. Copyright © 2003 by the President and Fellows of Harvard College.

To view copyright terms and conditions for Internet material cited here, log on to the home page for the referenced Web site.

During this book's preparation, all citations, facts, figures, names, addresses, telephone numbers, Internet URLs, and other pieces of information cited within were verified for accuracy. The authors and Saint Mary's Press staff have made every attempt to reference current and valid sources, but we cannot guarantee the content of any source, and we are not responsible for any changes that may have occurred since our verification. If you find an error in, or have a question or concern about, any of the information or sources listed within, please contact Saint Mary's Press.

Endnotes Cited in Quotations from the *Catechism of the Catholic Church*, Second Edition

1. *Dei Verbum* 11.
2. *Dei Verbum* 12 § 2.
3. *Dei Verbum* 25; cf. *Phil* 3:8 and St. Jerome, *Commentariorum in Isaiam libri xviii* prol.: Patrologia Latina 24, 17b.